Birds of New Jersey

Field Guide

by Stan Tekiela

Adventure Publications
Cambridge, Minnesota

TO MY WIFE KATHERINE AND DAUGHTER ABIGAIL WITH ALL MY LOVE

ACKNOWLEDGMENTS:

Special thanks to Anthony Hertzel for range maps, and New Jersey birders Vince Elia and Kevin T. Karlson for reviewing them. Special thanks also to Sandy Livoti for her exceptional eye to detail.

Book design and Illustrations by Jonathan Norberg

Photo credits by photographer and page number:

Cover photo: Eastern Bluebird by Maslowski Wildlife Productions **Brian Collins**: 2, 128, 172, 236, 244, 254 **Cornell Laboratory of Ornithology**: 70, 72 (female), 76 (perching), 216 (both) **Dudley Edmondson**: 18, 20, 44, 52 (soaring), 56, 58 (both), 78, 86, 92, 100 (both), 110, 112, 126 (in flight), 134 (both), 136 (male), 150 (soaring), 154, 164 (both), 168 (male), 170, 188 (male), 194 (breeding), 200, 208, 214 (male), 220 (both), 222, 226, 262, 266, 270, 282 (male), 284, 288 (male), 294 **Carrol Henderson**: 94 **Kevin T. Karlson**: 36, 40, 54 (juvenile), 118, 146 (both), 168 (female), 218, 264 (winter), 268, 278, 286 (female) **Bruce Leventhal**: 274 **Bill Marchel**: 4, 6, 26 (male), 28, 32, 72 (male), 84, 104, 106, 114, 130, 150 (perching), 156, 160, 174 (female), 188 (female), 192, 230, 232 (both), 238, 240, 246, 252, 260, 272, 276 **Maslowski Wildlife Productions**: 24, 74, 88, 108, 122, 178, 180, 186, 202, 256, 280, 290, 292 **Arthur Morris**: 46, 54 (breeding) **Steve Mortensen**: 8, 26 (female), 30 (both), 48 (both), 50, 52 (perching), 60, 62, 64, 66 (both), 80, 96, 98 (both), 158, 162, 182, 196, 198, 234, 282 (female), 298 (both) **Warren Nelson**: 10, 76 (soaring), 126 (perching), 136 (female), 288 (female) **John Pennoyer**: 82, 124, 242, 250, 300 **Brian E. Small**: 16, 38, 120, 140, 144, 148, 194 (winter), 204, 206, 248, 264 (breeding), 286 (male), 296 **Stan Tekiela**: 12, 14, 22 (both), 34 (both), 42, 68 (both), 90, 102 (both), 116, 132, 138, 142, 152, 166, 174 (male), 176, 184, 190, 210, 212, 214 (female), 228, 258 **Brian Wheeler**: 224 (both)

To the best of the publisher's knowledge, all photos but one were of live birds.

Second Printing

Published by Adventure Publications, Inc.
820 Cleveland St. S.
Cambridge, MN 55008
1-800-678-7006

Printed in China

Table of Contents

WHY WATCH BIRDS IN NEW JERSEY?

Millions of people have discovered bird feeding. It's a simple and enjoyable way to bring the beauty of birds closer to your home. Watching birds at your feeder often leads to a lifetime pursuit of bird identification. The *Birds of New Jersey Field Guide* is for those who want to identify common birds of New Jersey.

There are more than 800 species of birds found in North America. In New Jersey alone there have been over 440 different kinds of birds recorded over the years. These bird sightings were diligently recorded by hundreds of bird watchers and became part of the official state record. From these valuable records, I have chosen 122 of the most common birds of New Jersey to include in this field guide.

Bird watching, often called birding, is the largest spectator sport in America. Its outstanding popularity in New Jersey is due, in part, to an unusually rich and abundant birdlife. Why are there so many birds? One reason is open space. New Jersey is more than 8,000 square miles (21,000 sq. km), making it the forty-sixth largest state. Despite its small size, more than 8 million people call New Jersey home. That is about 1,000 people per square mile (400 per sq. km), half of whom are concentrated in and around 6 major cities. In fact, New Jersey is one of the most urban states since nearly 90 percent of its residents live in an urban setting. The concentrated urbanization in this state leaves plenty of room for a vast variety of birds.

The geography of New Jersey also plays a major role in migration. Each spring and autumn tens of thousands of shorebirds, ducks, geese and swans use the extensive marshes found along the Delaware River, Delaware Bay and Atlantic coast for feeding and resting. The freshwater lakes, bays and wetlands of northern New Jersey is another hot spot for birds. Thousands of hawks pass over Montclair Hawk Lookout, while a wide range of warblers can be seen passing through Cape May.

The state offers distinctly different habitats, each of which supports a different group of birds. The forested northern highlands and Kittatinny Mountains are home to birds such as the Great Crested Flycatcher. Long-legged shorebirds, such as the Sanderling, gravitate to the beaches of the Atlantic Ocean, while tiny bright-colored warblers, such as the American Redstart and Magnolia Warbler, flit amongst the pines in central New Jersey.

Whether witnessing a migration of hawks in the fall or welcoming back the hummingbirds in the spring, there is variety and excitement in birding in New Jersey.

OBSERVE WITH A STRATEGY; TIPS FOR IDENTIFYING BIRDS

Identifying birds isn't as difficult as you might think. If you follow just a few basic strategies, you can increase your chances of successfully identifying most birds you see! One of the first and easiest things to do when you see a new bird is to note its color. (Also, since this book is organized by color, you will go right to that color section to find it.)

Next, note the size of the bird. A strategy to quickly estimate size is to select a small-, medium- and large-sized bird to use for reference. For example, most people are familiar with robins. A robin, measured from the tip of its bill to the tip of its tail, is ten inches long. Using the robin as an example of a medium-sized bird, select two other birds, one smaller and one larger. Many people use a House Sparrow, at about 6 inches, and an American Crow, about 18 inches. When you see a bird that you don't know, you can quickly ask yourself, "Is it smaller than a robin, but larger than a sparrow?" When you look in your field guide to help identify your bird, you'll know it's roughly between six and ten inches long. This will help narrow your choices.

Next, note the size, shape and color of the bill. Is it long, thin, pointed, short, thick, blunt, curved or straight? Seed-eating birds, such as the Northern Cardinal, have bills that are thick and strong enough to crack even the toughest seeds. Birds that sip nectar, like Ruby-throated Hummingbirds, need long thin bills to reach deep into flowers. Hawks and owls tear their prey with very sharp, curved bills. Sometimes, just noting the bill shape can help you decide if the bird is a woodpecker, finch, grosbeak or blackbird.

Next, take a look around and note the habitat in which you see the bird. Is it wading in a marsh? Walking along a riverbank or on the beach? Soaring in the sky? Is it perched high in the trees or hopping along the forest floor? Because of their preferences in diet and habitat, you'll usually see robins hopping on the ground, but not often eating the seeds at your feeder. Or you'll see a Rose-breasted Grosbeak sitting on the branches of a tree, but not climbing down the tree trunk the way a nuthatch does.

Noticing what a bird is eating will give you another clue to help you identify that bird. Feeding is a big part of any bird's life. Fully one-third of all bird activities revolves around searching for and catching food, or actually eating. While birds don't always follow all the rules of what we think they eat, you can make some general assumptions. Northern Flickers, for instance, feed upon ants and other insects, so you wouldn't expect to see them visiting a backyard bird feeder. Some birds, such as Barn and Tree Swallows, feed on flying insects, and spend hours swooping and diving to catch a meal.

Sometimes you can identify a bird by the way it is perched. Body posture can help you to differentiate between an American Crow and a Red-tailed Hawk. American Crows lean forward over their feet when perched on a branch, while hawks perch in an upright or vertical position. Look for this the next time you see a large unidentified bird in a tree.

Birds in flight are often difficult to identify, but noting the size and shape of the wing will help. A bird's wing size is in direct proportion to its body size, weight and type of flying. The shape of the wing determines if the bird flies fast and with precision, or slowly and less precisely. Birds such as House Finches, which flit around a thick tangle of branches, have short round wings.

Birds that soar on warm updrafts of air, such as Turkey Vultures, have wings that are long and broad. Barn Swallows have short pointed wings that slice through the air, propelling their swift and accurate flight.

Some birds have unique flight patterns that aid in identification. American Goldfinches fly in a distinctive up-and-down pattern that makes it look as if they are riding a roller coaster.

While it's not easy to make these observations in the short time you often have to watch a "mystery bird," practicing these methods of identification will greatly expand your birding skills. Also, seek the guidance of a more experienced birder who will help you improve your skills and answer your questions on the spot.

BIRD BASICS

It's easier to identify birds and communicate about them if you know the names of the different parts of a bird. For instance, it's much easier to use the word "crest" to refer to the erect feathers on the head of a Northern Cardinal than trying to describe it.

The following illustration points out the basic parts of a bird. Because it's is a composite of many birds, it should not be confused with any actual bird.

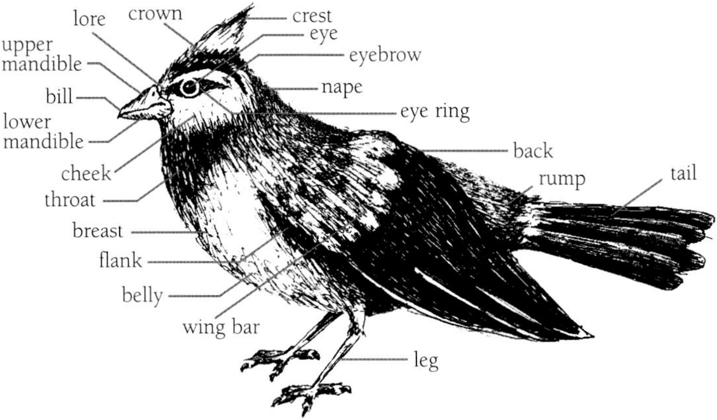

Bird Color Variables

No other animal has a color pallet like a bird's. Vivid blues, lemon yellows, intense reds and iridescent greens are commonplace within the bird world. In general, male birds are more colorful than their female counterparts. This is probably to help the male attract a mate, essentially saying, "Hey, look at me!" It also calls attention to the male's overall health. The better the condition of his feathers, the better his food source and territory, and therefore, the better his potential for a mate.

Females that don't look like their male counterparts (such species are called sexually dimorphic, meaning "two forms") are often a nondescript brown color, as seen with Rose-breasted Grosbeaks. These muted tones help to hide the females during weeks of motionless incubation, and draw less attention to her when she is out feeding or taking a break from the rigors of raising her young.

In some species, such as the Bald Eagle, Blue Jay and Downy Woodpecker, the male birds look nearly identical to the females. In the case of the woodpeckers, the sexes are only differentiated by a single red or sometimes yellow mark. Depending on the species, the mark may be on top of the head, face, nape of the neck or just behind the bill.

During the first year, juvenile birds often look like the mothers. Since brightly colored feathers are used mainly for attracting a mate, young non-breeding males don't have a need for colorful plumage. This also helps protect them while they are young. It is not until the first spring molt, or even several years later, depending on the species, that the young males obtain their breeding colors.

MOLTING

All birds molt. Molting is the process of dropping old worn feathers and replacing them with new ones. Typically, a bird will molt twice a year, with the first molt, or spring molt, usually occurring in late winter. During this molt the birds produce their breeding plumage (brighter colors for attracting mates), which will carry them through the summer. The second, or summer molt, serves two important functions. First, it adds additional feathers for warmth in the coming winter. Second, the winter plumage tends to be drab in color, such as that of the male American Goldfinch, which changes from canary yellow to olive brown. Luckily for us, some birds, such as the male Northern Cardinal, retain their bright summer color all year long.

Bird Nests

Bird nests are truly an amazing feat of engineering. Just imagine building your home strong enough to weather a storm, large enough to hold your entire family, warm enough to shelter them from the cold and waterproof enough to keep out rain. Now, build it without any blueprints or directions, and without the use of your hands or feet! Birds do!

Before building a nest, an appropriate site must be selected. With some birds, such as the House Wren, the male picks out several potential sites and assembles several small twigs in each. This discourages other birds from using nearby nest cavities. These "extra" nests are sometimes called dummy nests. The female is then taken around and shown all the choices. She chooses her favorite and finishes constructing the nest. With some other species of birds, for example, Baltimore Orioles, it's the female who chooses the site and builds the nest with the male only offering an occasional suggestion. Each bird species has its own nest-building routine, which is strictly followed.

Nesting material usually consists of natural elements found in the immediate area. Most nests consist of plant fibers (such as bark peeled from grapevines), sticks, mud, dried grass, feathers, fur, or soft fuzzy tufts from thistle. Some birds, including Ruby-throated Hummingbirds, use spider webs to glue nest materials together. Nesting material is limited to what a bird can hold or carry. Because of this, a bird must make many trips afield to gather enough materials to complete its nest. Most nests take at least four days or more, and hundreds, if not thousands, of trips to build.

As you'll see in the following illustrations, birds build a wide variety of nest types.

ground nest

platform nest

cup nest

pendulous nest

The simple **ground nest** is scraped out of the earth. These shallow depressions usually contain no nesting material, and are made by birds such as the Killdeer and Horned Lark.

Another type of nest, the **platform nest**, represents a more complex type of nest building. Constructed of small twigs and branches, the platform nest is a simple arrangement of sticks which forms a platform and features a small depression to nestle the eggs.

Some platform nests, such as those of the Common Loon, are constructed on the ground, and are made of mud and grass. Platform nests can also be on cliffs, bridges, balconies or even in flowerpots. This kind of nest gives space to adventurous youngsters, and functions as a landing platform for the parents. Many waterfowl construct platform nests on the ground, usually near water or actually in the water. These floating platform nests vary with the water level, thus preventing nests with eggs from being flooded. Platform nests, constructed by such birds as Mourning Doves and herons, are not anchored to the tree, and may tumble from the branches during high winds and storms

The **cup nest** is a modified platform nest, used by three-quarters of all songbirds. Constructed from the outside in, a supporting platform is constructed first. This platform is attached firmly to a tree, shrub or rock ledge. Next, the sides are constructed of grasses, small twigs, bark or leaves, which are woven together and often glued with mud for additional strength. The inner cup, lined with feathers, animal fur, soft plant material or animal hair, is constructed last. The mother bird uses her chest to cast the final contours of the inner nest.

The **pendulous nest** is an unusual nest, looking more like a sock hanging from a branch than a nest. Inaccessible to most predators, these nests are attached to the ends of the smallest branches of a tree, and often wave wildly in the breeze. Woven very tightly of plant fibers, they are strong and water tight, taking up to a week to build. More commonly used by tropical birds, this complicated nest type has also been mastered by orioles and kinglets. A small opening on the top or side allows the parents access to the grass-lined interior. (It must be one heck of a ride to be inside one of these nests during a windy spring thunderstorm!)

One of the most clever of all nest types is known as the **no nest** or daycare nest. Parasitic birds, like the Brown-headed Cowbird, build no nests at all! The egg-laden female expertly searches out other birds' nests and sneaks in to lay one of her own eggs while the host mother is not looking, thereby leaving the host mother to raise an adopted youngster. The mother cowbird wastes no energy building a nest only to have it raided by a predator. By using several nests of other birds, she spreads out her progeny in hope that at least one of her offspring will live to maturity.

Another nest type, the **cavity nest**, is used by many birds, including woodpeckers and Eastern Bluebirds. The cavity nest is usually excavated in a tree branch or trunk, and offers shelter from the storms, sun, predators and the cold of New Jersey's climate. A relatively small entrance hole in a tree leads to an inner chamber up to ten inches below. In some cases, a four-foot tunnel connects the entrance in a riverbank to the nest chamber. These nests are often sparsely lined because they are well insulated. Usually constructed by woodpeckers and kingfishers, the cavity nest is used only once by its builder, but can be used for many years by birds such as the Common Goldeneye, mergansers and bluebirds, which do not have the capability of excavating one for themselves.

Some birds, including some swallows, take nest building one step further. They use a collection of small balls of mud to construct an adobe-style home. Constructed under the eaves of houses, under bridges or inside chimneys, some of these nests look like simple cup nests. Others are completely enclosed, with small tunnel-like openings that lead into a safe nesting chamber for the baby birds.

Who Builds the Nest?

In general, the female bird builds the nest. She gathers nesting materials and constructs a nest, with an occasional visit from her mate to check on the progress. In some species, both parents contribute equally to the construction of a nest. A male bird might forage for precisely the right sticks, grass or mud, but it's often the female that forms or puts together the nest. She uses her body to form the egg chamber. Rarely does the male build a nest by himself.

Fledging

Fledging is the interval between hatching and flight or leaving the nest. Some birds leave the nest within hours of hatching, but it might be weeks before they are able to fly. This is common with waterfowl. Until they start to fly, they are called fledglings. Birds that are still in the nest are called nestlings.

Why Birds Migrate

Why do birds migrate? The short answer is simple–food. Birds migrate to areas of high food concentrations. It is easier to breed where food is than where it is not. A typical migrating bird, the Rose-breasted Grosbeak, for instance, migrates from the tropics of Central and South America to nest in the forests of North America, taking advantage of billions of newly hatched insects to feed its young. This trip is called **complete migration**.

Some birds of prey return from their complete migration to northern regions that are overflowing with small rodents, such as mice and voles, that have continued to breed in winter.

Complete migrators have a set time and pattern of migration. Each year at nearly the same time, they take off and head for a specific wintering ground. Complete migrators may travel incredible distances, sometimes as much as 15,000 miles or more in one year. But complete migration doesn't necessarily imply flying from the cold and frozen northland to some tropical destination. Dark-eyed Junco, for example, is a complete migrator that flies from the far reaches of Canada to spend the winter right here in cold and snowy New Jersey.

There are many interesting aspects to complete migrators. In the spring, males usually migrate several weeks before the females, arriving early to scope out possible nesting sites and food sources, and to begin to defend territories. The females arrive several weeks later. In the autumn, in many species, the females and their young leave early, often up to four weeks before the adult males.

Not all migrators are the same. There are **partial migrators**, such as American Goldfinches, that usually wait until food supplies dwindle before they fly south. Unlike complete migrators, the partial migrators move only far enough south, or sometimes east and west, to find abundant food. Some years it might be only a few hundred miles, while other years it might be nearly a thousand. This kind of migration, dependent upon the weather and available food, is sometimes called **seasonal movement**.

Unlike the predictable ebbing and flowing behavior of the complete migrators or partial migrators, **irruptive migrators** can move every third to fifth year, or in some cases, in consecutive years. These migrations are triggered when times are really tough and food is scarce. Red-breasted Nuthatches are a good example of irruptive migrators, because they leave their normal northern range in search of food or in response to overpopulation.

How Do Birds Migrate?

One of the many secrets of migration is fat. While we humans are fighting the battle of the bulge, birds intentionally gorge themselves to put on as much fat as possible while still being able to fly. Fat provides the greatest amount of energy per unit of weight, and in the same way that your car needs gas, birds are propelled by fat or stalled without it.

During long migratory flights, fat deposits are used up quickly, and birds need to stop to "refuel." This is when backyard bird feeding stations and undeveloped, natural spaces around our towns and cities are especially important. Some birds require up to two to three days of constant feeding to build up their fat reserves before continuing their seasonal trip.

Some birds, such as most eagles, hawks, osprey, falcons, and vultures, migrate during the day. Larger birds can hold more body fat, go longer without eating, and take longer to migrate. These birds glide along on rising columns of warm air called thermals, which hold them aloft while they slowly make their way south. They generally rest at night and hunt early in the morning before the sun has a chance to warm up the land and create good soaring conditions. Birds migrating during the day use a combination of landforms, rivers, and the rising and setting setting sun to guide them in the right direction.

Most birds migrate during the night. Studies show that birds which migrate at night use the stars to navigate. Others use the setting sun, while still others, such as doves, use the earth's magnetic fields to guide them south. While flying at night might seem like a crazy idea, nocturnal migration is safer for several reasons. First, there are fewer nighttime predators for migrating birds. Second, traveling at night allows time during the day to find food in unfamiliar surroundings. Finally, nighttime wind patterns tend to be flat, or laminar. These flat winds don't have the turbulence associated with daytime winds, and can actually help carry smaller birds by pushing them along.

HOW TO USE THIS GUIDE

To help you quickly and easily identify birds, this book is organized by color. Simply note the color of the bird and turn to that section. Refer to the first page for the color key. The male Rose-breasted Grosbeak, for example, is black-and-white with a red patch on its chest. Because the bird is mostly black and white, it will be found in the black and white section. Each color section is also arranged by size, generally with the smaller birds first. Sections may also incorporate the average size in a range, which in some cases reflects size differences between male and female birds. Flip through the pages in that color section to find the bird. If you already know the name of the bird, check the index for the page number. In some species, the male and female are remarkably different in color. In these cases, the opposite sex is shown in a smaller inset photograph with a page reference. These birds, therefore, will be found in two different color sections.

In the description section you will find a variety of information about the bird. On the following page is a sample of the information included in the book.

Range Maps

Range maps are included for each bird. The colored areas indicate where in New Jersey a particular bird is most likely to be found. Green is used for summer, blue for winter, red for year-round and yellow for areas where the bird is seen during migration. While every effort has been made to accurately depict these ranges, they are only general guidelines. Ranges actually change on an ongoing basis due to a variety of factors. Changes in weather, species abundance, landscape and vital resources such as the availability of food and water can affect local populations, migration and movements, causing birds to be found in areas not typical for the species.

The colored areas simply mean bird sightings for that species have been frequent in those areas and less frequent in the others. Please use the maps as intended–as general guides only.

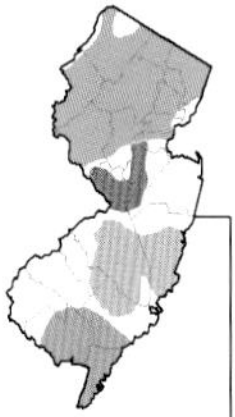

COMMON NAME
Scientific name

SAMPLE PAGE

COLOR INDICATOR

Size: measured from head to tail

Male: a brief description of the male bird

Female: a brief description of the female bird, which is sometimes not the same as the male

Juvenile: a brief description of the juvenile bird, which often looks like the female

Nest: the kind of nest this bird builds to raise its young, who builds the nest, and how many broods per year

Eggs: how many eggs you might expect to see in a nest, and the color of the eggs

Incubation: the average time the parents spend incubating the eggs, and who does the incubation

Fledging: the average time the young spend in the nest after hatching but before they leave the nest, and which parent(s) does most of the "child-care" and feeding

Migration: type of migration: complete (consistent, seasonal), or partial (seasonal, destination varies), or irruptive (unpredictable, depending on the food supply), or non-migrator (the general location where the bird spends the winter)

Food: what the bird eats most of the time (e.g., seeds, nectar, insects, fruit, small animals), and if it typically comes to a bird feeding station

Compare: notes about other birds that look similar, and the pages on which they can be found

Stan's Notes: Interesting gee-whiz natural history information. This could be something to look or listen for, or something to help positively identify the bird. Also includes remarkable features.

female
pg. 109
male

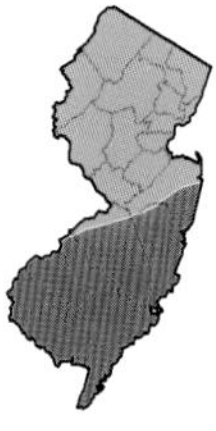

YEAR-ROUND
SUMMER

EASTERN TOWHEE
Pipilo erythrophthalmus

Size: 7-8" (18-20 cm)

Male: A mostly black bird with dirty red brown sides and white belly. Long black tail with white tip. Short, stout, pointed bill with rich red eye. White wing patches flash in flight.

Female: similar to male, but is brown, not black

Juvenile: light brown, heavily streaked head, chest, and belly, long dark tail with white tip

Nest: cup; female builds; 2 broods per year

Eggs: 3-4; creamy white with brown markings

Incubation: 12-13 days; female incubates

Fledging: 10-12 days; female and male feed young

Migration: complete, to southern states and South America

Food: insects, seeds, fruit, comes to ground feeder

Compare: Slightly smaller than the American Robin (pg. 215). The Gray Catbird (pg. 211) lacks a black "hood" and rusty sides. Common Grackle (pg. 11) lacks white belly and has long thin bill. Male Rose-breasted Grosbeak (pg. 29) has a rosy patch in center of chest.

Stan's Notes: Common name comes from its distinctive "tow-hee" call given by both sexes. Mostly known for its characteristic call that sounds like, "Drink-your-tea!" White-eyed form in southern states. Seen hopping backward with both feet to rake up leaf litter, called bilateral scratching, in search of insects and seeds. Female broods, but male does most of the feeding of young.

female pg. 113
male

Brown-headed Cowbird
Molothrus ater

Size: 7½" (19 cm)

Male: A glossy black bird, reminiscent of a Red-winged Blackbird. Chocolate brown head with a pointed, sharp gray bill.

Female: dull brown bird with bill similar to male

Juvenile: similar to female, only duller gray with streaked chest

Nest: no nest; lays eggs in nests of other birds

Eggs: 5-7; white with brown markings

Incubation: 10-13 days; host bird incubates eggs

Fledging: 10-11 days; host birds feed young

Migration: complete, to southern states

Food: insects, seeds, will come to seed feeders

Compare: In the blackbird family. The slightly larger male Red-winged Blackbird (pg. 9) has red and yellow markings on wings. Common Grackle (pg. 11) has a long tail, but lacks brown head. European Starling (pg. 7) has yellow bill and shorter tail.

Stan's Notes: Of about 750 species of parasitic birds worldwide, this is the only parasitic bird in New Jersey, laying all eggs in host birds' nests, leaving others to raise its young. Cowbirds are known to have laid eggs in nests of over 200 species of birds. Some birds reject cowbird eggs, but most raise them, even to the exclusion of their own young. Look for warblers and other birds feeding young birds twice their own size. At one time they followed bison to feed on the insects attracted to the animals.

European Starling
Sturnus vulgaris

YEAR-ROUND

Size: 7½" (19 cm)

Male: An iridescent purple black bird covered with white speckles during fall and winter. Shiny purple black in spring and summer. Long, pointed gray bill in autumn and yellow in spring. Short tail.

Female: same as male

Juvenile: similar to adult, only gray brown with streaked chest

Nest: cavity; male and female line cavity; 2 broods per year

Eggs: 4-6; bluish with brown markings

Incubation: 12-14 days; female and male incubate

Fledging: 18-20 days; female and male feed young

Migration: non-migrator to partial migrator, some will move to southern states

Food: insects, seeds, fruit, will come to seed and suet feeders

Compare: Looks similar to Common Grackle (pg. 11), but lacks its long tail.

Stan's Notes: Great songsters, they are also able to mimic sounds. Often displaces woodpeckers, chickadees and other cavity-nesting birds. Can be very aggressive and destroy eggs or young of other birds. The bill changes color with the seasons: yellow in spring and gray in autumn. Jaws are designed to be most powerful when opening, as they pry open crevices to locate hidden insects. Gathers in the hundreds in autumn. Not a native bird, they were introduced to New York City in 1890-91 from Europe.

female pg. 125
male

RED-WINGED BLACKBIRD

Agelaius phoeniceus

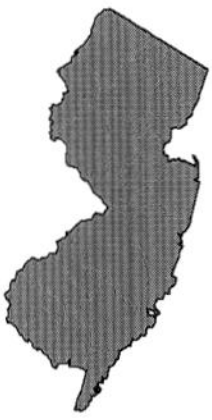

YEAR-ROUND

Size: 8½" (22 cm)

Male: Jet black bird with red and yellow shoulder patch on upper wing. Pointed black bill.

Female: heavily streaked brown bird with white eyebrow, brown bill

Juvenile: same as female

Nest: cup; female builds; 2-3 broods per year

Eggs: 3-4; bluish green with brown markings

Incubation: 10-12 days; female incubates

Fledging: 11-14 days; female and male feed young

Migration: complete, to southern states, Mexico and Central America

Food: insects, seeds, will come to seed feeders

Compare: Slightly larger than the male Brown-headed Cowbird (pg. 5), but is less iridescent and lacks Cowbird's brown head. Differs from all blackbirds due to the red and yellow patches on its wings, called epaulets.

Stan's Notes: It is a sure sign of spring when the Red-winged Blackbirds return to the marsh. Flocks of up to 100,000 birds have been reported. Males return before females and defend territories. Will repeat call from top of cattail while showing off red and yellow wing bars, called epaulets. Females choose mate. Nests are usually over shallow water in thick stand of cattails. One of the most widespread and numerous birds in New Jersey. Feeds mostly on seeds in spring and fall, switching to insects during summer.

YEAR-ROUND

COMMON GRACKLE
Quiscalus quiscula

Size: 11-13" (28-33 cm)

Male: Large black bird with iridescent blue black head, purple brown body, long black tail, long thin bill and bright golden eyes.

Female: similar to male, only duller and smaller

Juvenile: similar to female

Nest: cup; female builds; 2 broods per year

Eggs: 4-5; greenish white with brown markings

Incubation: 13-14 days; female incubates

Fledging: 16-20 days; female and male feed young

Migration: complete, to southern states

Food: fruit, seeds, insects, comes to seed feeders

Compare: European Starling (pg. 7) is much smaller and has a speckled appearance and yellow bill. Male Red-winged Blackbird (pg. 9) has red and yellow wing markings.

Stan's Notes: Usually nests in small colonies of up to 75 pairs. Travels with other blackbirds in large flocks. Known to feed in farmers' fields. Their name comes from the Latin word *graculus*, meaning "to cough," for their loud raspy call. They hold their tails in a keel-like position during flight. Flight pattern is almost always level, as opposed to undulated up-and-down movements. Unlike most birds, has larger muscles to open mouth rather than to close it, as it pries open crevices to locate hidden insects.

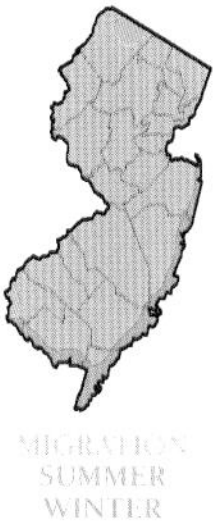

American Coot
Fulica americana

Size: 13-16" (33-40 cm)

Male: Slate gray-to-black all over, white bill with dark band near tip. Green legs and feet. Small white patch near the base of tail. Prominent red eye and a small red patch above bill between eyes.

Female: same as male

Juvenile: much paler than adult, with a gray bill and same white rump patch

Nest: floating platform; female and male build; 1 brood per year

Eggs: 9-12; pinkish buff with brown markings

Incubation: 21-25 days; female and male incubate

Fledging: 49-52 days; female and male feed young

Migration: complete, to southern states and Central America

Food: insects, aquatic plants

Compare: Smaller than most waterfowl, it is the only black water bird or duck-like bird with a white bill.

Stan's Notes: An excellent diver and swimmer often seen in large flocks on open water. Not a duck, as they don't have webbed feet, but instead have large lobed toes. When taking off, they scramble across the surface of the water with wings flapping. Look for them bobbing their heads while swimming. Huge flocks of up to 1,000 birds gather for fall migration. Its unusual name is of unknown origin, but in Middle English, *coote* was used to describe various waterfowl–perhaps it stuck. Nest is floating mat of vegetation.

male
female pg. 145

YEAR-ROUND

Boat-tailed Grackle
Quiscalus major

Size: 16" (40 cm), male
14" (36 cm), female

Male: Iridescent blue-black bird with a very long keel-shaped tail. Bright yellow eye.

Female: brown version of male, lacking any iridescence

Juvenile: similar to adult

Nest: cup; female builds; 2 broods per year

Eggs: 2-4; pale greenish blue, brown markings

Incubation: 13-15 days; female incubates

Fledging: 12-15 days; female feeds young

Migration: non-migrator, moves around to find food

Food: insects, berries, seeds, fish

Compare: The male Boat-tailed Grackle is similar to the male Common Grackle (pg. 11), but the Boat-tailed has a distinctive long tail.

Stan's Notes: A bird of coastal saltwater marshes, it has only recently expanded its range into New Jersey in the last 40 years. A noisy bird that gives several harsh, high-pitched calls and several squeaks. Nests in small colonies. Boat-taileds on the Gulf coast have dark eyes, while the Atlantic coast birds have bright yellow eyes. Eats a wide variety of foods from grains to fish. Sometimes seen picking insects off backs of cattle. Will also visit bird feeders. Makes a cup nest with mud or cow dung.

Fish Crow
Corvus ossifragus

YEAR-ROUND

Size: 16" (40 cm)

Male: All-black bird appearing nearly very similar to the American Crow, but with longer tail, and a smaller head and bill.

Female: same as male

Juvenile: same as adult

Nest: cup; female and male build; 1 brood per year

Eggs: 4-5; blue or gray-green, brown markings

Incubation: 16-18 days; female and male incubate

Fledging: 21-24 days; female and male feed young

Migration: non-migrator

Food: aquatic insects, carrion, berries, seeds

Compare: Nearly identical to American Crow (pg. 19), but the Fish Crow is smaller, has a longer tail, and a smaller head and bill. Fish Crow is most easily differentiated by its higher pitched call.

Stan's Notes: The Fish Crow numbers have been expanding in New Jersey. Essentially a bird of the coastal tidewaters and along major rivers, but can now be found nearly throughout the state. Not uncommon for it to break open mollusk shells by dropping onto rocks from above. Forms small winter flocks of up to 100 birds, unlike the American Crow, which often forms winter flocks of several hundred. Very sociable and gregarious. Nests in small colonies, often building a stick nest halfway up cedar trees.

AMERICAN CROW
Corvus brachyrhynchos

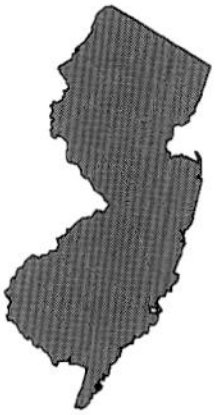

YEAR-ROUND

Size: 18" (45 cm)

Male: All-black bird with black bill, legs and feet. Can have purple sheen in direct sunlight.

Female: same as male

Juvenile: same as adult

Nest: platform; female builds; 1 brood per year

Eggs: 4-6; bluish to olive green, brown markings

Incubation: 18 days; female incubates

Fledging: 28-35 days; female and male feed young

Migration: non-migrator to partial migrator

Food: fruit, insects, mammals, fish, carrion, will come to seed and suet feeders

Compare: Nearly identical to the Fish Crow (pg. 17), but American Crow is larger, has a shorter tail, and a larger head and bill. American Crow is most easily differentiated by its lower pitched call.

Stan's Notes: One of the most recognizable birds in New Jersey. Often reuse nest every year if not taken over by a Great Horned Owl. They collect and store bright, shiny objects in the nest. Able to mimic human voices, and other birds. One of the smartest of all birds, they are very social, often entertaining themselves by provoking chases with other birds. They feed on road kill but are rarely hit by cars. Can live up to 20 years. Unmated birds, known as helpers, help raise young. Large extended families roost together at night, then disperse during the day to hunt.

YEAR-ROUND

Turkey Vulture
Cathartes aura

Size: 26-32" (66-80 cm); up to 6-foot wingspan

Male: Large bird with obvious red head and legs. When seen overhead, wings appear two-toned, black leading edge with gray on trailing edge and tip. Tip of wings end in finger-like projections. Squared-off tail. Ivory bill.

Female: same as male

Juvenile: same as adult, but often has a gray-to-blackish head and bill

Nest: no nest, or minimal nest on cliff or in cave; 1 brood per year

Eggs: 2; white with brown markings

Incubation: 38-41 days; female and male incubate

Fledging: 66-88 days; female and male feed young

Migration: complete, to southern states, Central and South Americas

Food: carrion, parents regurgitate for young

Compare: Smaller than the Bald Eagle (pg. 59), look for Vulture's two-toned colored wings. Flies holding wings in a slight V shape, unlike the straight wing position of the Eagle.

Stan's Notes: Vultures' naked heads are an adaptation to reduce the risk of feather fouling (picking up diseases) from carcasses. Unlike hawks and eagles, they have weak feet more suited to walking than grasping. One of the few birds with a developed sense of smell. They're generally mute, making only grunts or groans. Groups often seen in trees with wings outstretched to catch sun.

DOUBLE-CRESTED CORMORANT
Phalacrocorax auritus

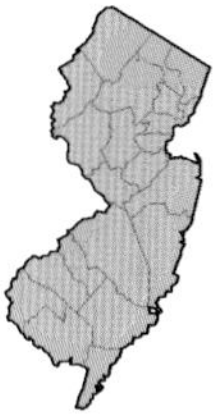

MIGRATION
SUMMER

Size: 33" (84 cm)

Male: Large all-black water bird with long snake-like neck. Long yellow orange bill with hooked tip.

Female: same as male

Juvenile: lighter brown with grayish-colored neck and breast

Nest: platform nest in colony; male and female build; 1 brood per year

Eggs: 3-4; bluish white, unmarked

Incubation: 25-29 days; female and male incubate

Fledging: 37-42 days; male and female feed young

Migration: complete, to southern states, Mexico and Central America

Food: small fish, aquatic insects

Compare: Same size as Loon (pg. 57), but Cormorant has longer neck and yellow bill, lacking black-and-white checker pattern of Loon.

Stan's Notes: Often seen flying in large V formation. Often roost in large groups in trees near water. Catches fish by swimming with wings held at its sides. To dry off they strike an erect pose with wings outstretched facing the sun. Their name refers to the nearly invisible crest on their heads. "Cormorant" comes from the Latin word *corvus*, meaning "crow," and *L. marinus*, meaning "pertaining to the sea," literally, "Sea Crow."

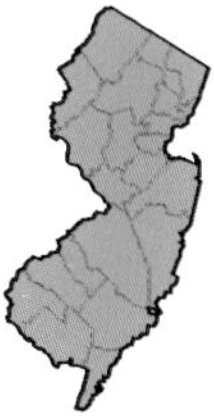

SUMMER

Black-and-white Warbler
Mniotilta varia

Size: 5" (13 cm)

Male: Striped like a zebra, this small warbler has a white belly and black chin with distinctive black-and-white stripes on crown and black cheek patch.

Female: same as male, only duller and without the black chin and cheek patch

Juvenile: similar to female

Nest: cup; female builds; 1 brood per year

Eggs: 4-5; white with brown markings

Incubation: 10-11 days; female incubates

Fledging: 9-12 days; female and male feed young

Migration: complete, to Central and South Americas

Food: insects

Compare: Watch for Black-and-white Warbler creeping down a tree trunk like White-breasted Nuthatch (pg. 193).

Stan's Notes: One of the first warblers to return each spring. Look for this common warbler searching for insect eggs in the bark of large trees. The female will perform a distraction dance to draw predators away from nest. It is the only warbler that moves head-first down a tree trunk. Song sounds like a slowly turning, squeaky wheel. Makes nest on the ground concealed under dead leaves.

male
female

Downy Woodpecker
Picoides pubescens

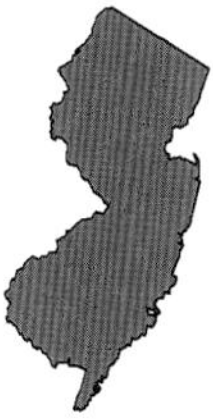

YEAR-ROUND

Size: 6" (15 cm)

Male: A small woodpecker with all-white belly, black-and-white spotted wings, a black line running through its eyes, a short black bill, a white stripe down back and a red mark on nape of neck. Several small black spots along side of white tail.

Female: same as male, lacking red mark on nape

Juvenile: same as female, some juveniles can have a red mark near forehead

Nest: cavity; male and female excavate cavity; 1 brood per year

Eggs: 3-5; white, unmarked

Incubation: 11-12 days; female and male incubate, female during day, male at night

Fledging: 20-25 days; male and female feed young

Migration: non-migrator

Food: insects, will come to seed and suet feeders

Compare: Almost identical to the Hairy Woodpecker (pg. 31), but smaller. Look for the shorter, thinner bill of Downy to differentiate them.

Stan's Notes: Both sexes will drum on a hollow log or branch to announce territories. Males perform most brooding and incubate all night. One of the most abundant woodpeckers. Small percentage of young will have a red spot on crown. Stiff tail feathers help brace the bird, like a tripod, as it clings to a tree branch. All woodpeckers have long barbed tongues, used to pull insects out of tiny places. Will winter roost in cavity.

female
pg. 115
male

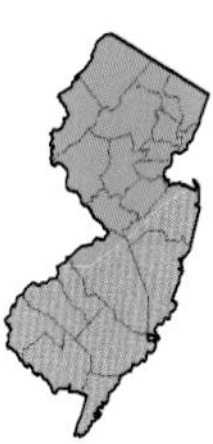

MIGRATION
SUMMER

Rose-breasted Grosbeak
Pheucticus ludovicianus

Size: 7-8" (18-20 cm)

Male: Plump black-and-white bird with large, triangular rose patch on center of chest. Wing linings are rosy red. Large ivory bill.

Female: heavily streaked brown and white with large white eyebrow line, wing linings are orange yellow

Juvenile: same as female

Nest: cup; female and male build; 1-2 broods per year

Eggs: 3-5; blue green with brown markings

Incubation: 13-14 days; female and male incubate

Fledging: 9-12 days; female and male feed young

Migration: complete, to Mexico, Central and South Americas

Food: insects, seeds, fruit, comes to seed feeders

Compare: Males are very distinctive with no look-alikes. Females look like large sparrows. Female is larger and has more distinctive eyebrow mark than female Purple Finch (pg. 97). Female House Finch (pg. 83) has no eyebrow mark.

Stan's Notes: Both males and females sing, but males sing much louder and clearer. Rich robin-like song. White wing patches flash when in flight. The name "Grosbeak" refers to its large bill, used to crush seeds. Male's red breast patch varies in size and shape in each individual. Males arrive first in spring, joined by females several days later. Late to arrive in spring and early to leave in autumn.

female

YEAR-ROUND

Hairy Woodpecker

Picoides villosus

Size: 9" (22.5 cm)

Male: Black-and-white woodpecker with a white belly and black wings with rows of white spots. White stripe down back. Long black bill. Red mark on back of head.

Female: same as male, lacks red spot

Juvenile: grayer version of adult, lacks red spot

Nest: cavity; female and male excavate hole; 1 brood per year

Eggs: 3-6; white, unmarked

Incubation: 11-15 days; female and male incubate, female during day, male at night

Fledging: 28-30 days; male and female feed young

Migration: non-migrator

Food: insects, seeds, nuts, will come to seed and suet feeders

Compare: Larger than Downy Woodpecker (pg. 27), Hairy has a longer bill and lacks Downy's black spots along tail.

Stan's Notes: A common backyard bird that announces its arrival with a sharp chirp before landing on feeders. Has tiny bristle-like feathers at base of bill to protect nostrils from wood dust. Barbed tongue helps extract insects from trees. Drums on hollow logs, branches or stovepipes in spring to announce territory. Responsible for eating many destructive forest insects. Often prefers to excavate nest cavities in live aspen trees. Has a large, more oval-shaped cavity entrance than that of Downy Woodpecker.

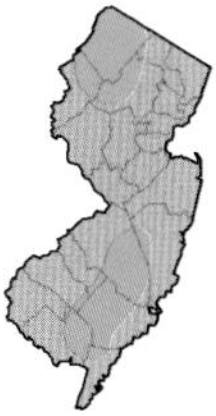

MIGRATION
SUMMER

Red-headed Woodpecker
Melanerpes erythrocephalus

Size: 9" (22.5 cm)

Male: All-red head and solid black back. White rump, chest and belly. Has large white patches on wings that flash when in flight. Black tail. Gray legs and bill.

Female: same as male

Juvenile: gray brown with white chest, lacking any red

Nest: cavity; male builds with help from female; 1 brood per year

Eggs: 4-5; white, unmarked

Incubation: 12-13 days; female and male incubate

Fledging: 27-30 days; female and male feed young

Migration: partial migrator, moves around to areas with abundant supply of nuts

Food: insects, fruit, nuts, comes to seed and suet feeders

Compare: No other New Jersey woodpecker has an all-red head. Pileated Woodpecker (pg. 49) is the only other woodpecker with a solid black back, but has a partial red head.

Stan's Notes: Bill is not as well adapted for excavating holes as in other woodpeckers, so it chooses dead or rotten tree branches for nest. Later nesting than the closely related Red-bellied Woodpecker, and will often take over its nest cavity. Prefers more open or edge woodland with many dead trees. Often seen perching on tops of dead snags. Stores acorns and other nuts.

male
female

YEAR-ROUND

Red-bellied Woodpecker
Melanerpes carolinus

Size: 9¼" (23 cm)

Male: "Zebra-backed" woodpecker with a white rump. Red crown extends down the nape of neck. Tan breast with a tinge of red on belly, which is often hard to see.

Female: same as male, with gray crown

Juvenile: gray version of adult, no red crown or nape

Nest: cavity; female and male build; 1 brood per year

Eggs: 4-5; white, unmarked

Incubation: 12-14 days; female and male incubate, female during day, male at night

Fledging: 24-27 days; female and male feed young

Migration: non-migrator

Food: insects, nuts, fruit, will come to seed and suet feeders

Compare: Similar to Northern Flicker (pg. 137). Note tan chest and belly with obvious stripes on back. The Red-headed Woodpecker (pg. 33) has an all-red head.

Stan's Notes: Mostly a bird of shady woodland, it excavates holes in rotten wood looking for spiders, centipedes and beetles. Often kicked out of nest hole by European Starlings. Will return to same tree to excavate a new nest below that of previous year. Hammers acorns and berries into crevices of trees for winter food.

winter pg. 219
breeding

WINTER

Black-bellied Plover
Pluvialis squatarola

Size: 11-12" (28-30 cm)

Male: Black legs and bill. Striking black and white breeding plumage, with a frosty white cap and nape of neck. Black face, neck, chest and sides. Winter plumage is light gray with fine streaks on belly.

Female: less black on chest and belly than male

Juvenile: grayer than adult, with much less black

Nest: ground; male and female build; 1 brood per year

Eggs: 3-4; pinkish or greenish with black-brown markings

Incubation: 26-27 days; male and female incubate, male during day, female at night

Fledging: 35-45 days; male feeds young, young learn quickly to feed themselves

Migration: complete, to East and Gulf coasts, West Indies to the coast of South America

Food: insects

Compare: Slightly larger than the Dunlin (pg. 121), and lacking its rusty back and long downward-curved bill. Look for frosty white head and extensive black patch on face, chest and belly.

Stan's Notes: Males perform a "butterfly" courtship flight to attract females. Female leaves male and young 12 days after eggs hatch. Breeds at age three. Begins migration in July and August. In flight, in any plumage, Plover displays white rump and stripe on wing with black axillaries (armpit). Often darts across ground to grab an insect and run.

female pg. 141
male

Bufflehead
Bucephala albeola

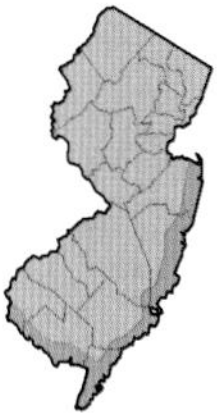

MIGRATION
WINTER

Size: 13-15" (33-38 cm)

Male: A small duck with striking white sides and black back. Green purple head with large white bonnet-like patch.

Female: brown version of male, with brown head and white patch on cheek, just behind eye

Juvenile: similar to female

Nest: cavity; female lines former woodpecker cavity; 1 brood per year

Eggs: 8-10; ivory to olive without markings

Incubation: 29-31 days; female incubates

Fledging: 50-55 days; female leads young to food

Migration: complete, to southern states and Central America

Food: aquatic insects

Compare: Male Bufflehead commonly confused with male Hooded Merganser (pg. 43), which lacks Bufflehead's white sides. The male Common Goldeneye (pg. 51) is slightly larger than Bufflehead and shares white sides and black back, but lacks the large white head patch.

Stan's Notes: A common diving duck, Buffleheads travel amongst other ducks. Most commonly found in sheltered bays and coastal harbors, it is also found inland on rivers and lakes. Doesn't nest in New Jersey. Unlike other ducks, young remain in nests for up to two days before venturing out with their mothers. Female is very territorial and remains with the same mate for many years.

female pg. 149
male

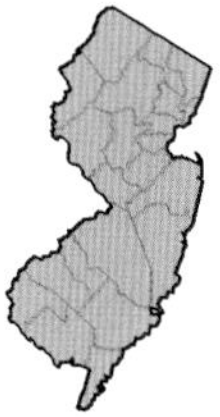

MIGRATION

Lesser Scaup
Aythya affinis

Size: 16-17" (40-43 cm)

Male: Appears mostly black with bold white sides and gray back. Chest and head look nearly black but in sun, head appears purple with green highlights. Bright yellow eye.

Female: overall brown with a dull white patch near base of bill

Juvenile: same as female

Nest: ground; female builds; 1 brood per year

Eggs: 8-14; olive buff without markings

Incubation: 22-28 days; female incubates

Fledging: 45-50 days; female teaches young to feed

Migration: complete, to the southern states, northern South America, Central America

Food: aquatic plants and insects

Compare: The male Lesser Scaup is nearly identical to the slightly larger, but less common, male Greater Scaup (pg. 45).

Stan's Notes: A common diving duck in New Jersey. Often seen in large flocks numbering in the thousands on area lakes, ponds and sewage lagoons. Usually only seen during migrations in late February and again in October. When observed in flight, note the bold white stripe under the wings. Has an interesting baby-sitting arrangement in which the young form groups tended by one to three adult females.

female pg. 153
male

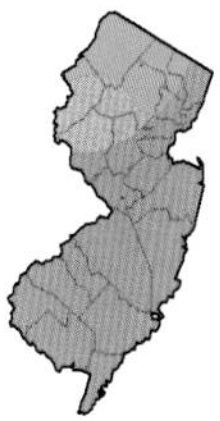

HOODED MERGANSER
Lophodytes cucullatus

Size: 16-19" (40-48 cm)

Male: A sleek black-and-white bird with rusty brown sides. Crest "hood" raises to reveal large white patch. Long, thin black bill.

Female: sleek brown and rust bird with a ragged rusty crest and long, thin brown bill

Juvenile: similar to female

Nest: cavity; female lines former woodpecker hole; 1 brood per year

Eggs: 10-12; white, unmarked

Incubation: 32-33 days; female incubates

Fledging: 71 days; female feeds young

Migration: complete, to Gulf coast and Mexico

Food: small fish, aquatic insects

Compare: Smaller than the male Common Merganser (pg. 241). Look for a large white patch on "hood" and rusty sides.

Stan's Notes: Not as common as the Common Merganser, the male Hooded Merganser can voluntarily raise and lower the crest on its head to show off the large white patch. Females will "dump" eggs into other female Hooded Mergansers' nests, resulting in 20 to 25 eggs in some nests. Mergansers have been known to share a nesting cavity with Common Goldeneyes and Wood Ducks sitting side by side.

female pg. 155
male

Greater Scaup
Aythya marila

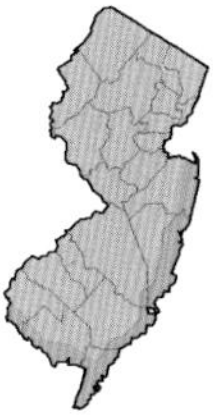

MIGRATION
WINTER

Size: 18" (45 cm)

Male: Black head shines green in direct light. Has bright white sides and gray back. Light blue bill with a black tip. Rounded head.

Female: brown with a darker head and a bold white patch at base of bill, might show a white patch just behind eye, top of head rounded

Juvenile: similar to adult

Nest: ground; female builds; 1 brood per year

Eggs: 7-10; greenish-olive, unmarked

Incubation: 24-28 days; female incubates

Fledging: 45-50 days; female teaches young to feed

Migration: complete, along East and Gulf coasts

Food: aquatic plants and insects

Compare: Very similar to male Lesser Scaup (pg. 41), only slightly larger. Has a rounded head vs. the Lesser's more pointed head. The male Greater Scaup has a larger black mark on tip of bill.

Stan's Notes: Can be one of the most common ducks during winter in coastal New Jersey. They arrive in early October, leave by mid-April and don't nest in the state. With a ratio of about ten to one, Greater Scaups are by far more common than Lesser Scaups. Greater Scaups prefer saltwater, while the Lesser Scaups seem to prefer fresh water. Most abundant on large saltwater bays. Breeds in northern Canada and Alaska.

YEAR-ROUND

American Oystercatcher
Haematopus palliatus

Size: 18-19" (45-48 cm)

Male: A large shorebird with large red-orange bill, black head and dark brown sides, wings and back. White chest and belly, pink legs and a red ring around the eyes.

Female: same as male

Juvenile: more gray than black and lacking the brightly colored bill

Nest: ground; male and female build; 1 brood per year

Eggs: 2-4; olive with sparse brown markings

Incubation: 24-29 days; male and female incubate, male during day, female at night

Fledging: 35-40 days; male and female feed young, young learn quickly to feed themselves

Migration: complete, to East and Gulf coasts, West Indies to the coast of South America

Food: shellfish, insects, aquatic insects, worms

Compare: Larger than Black-bellied Plover (pg. 37). Look for the large and obvious red-orange bill of the Oystercatcher to identify.

Stan's Notes: A large, chunky shorebird with a flattened, heavy bill, used to pry open shellfish and to probe in the sand for insects and worms. The birds can be categorized according to their preferred oyster-opening technique. Stabbers sneak up on mollusks and stab their bills between the shells before they have a chance to close. Hammerers shatter one-half of the shell with several direct, powerful blows.

male
female

Pileated Woodpecker
Dryocopus pileatus

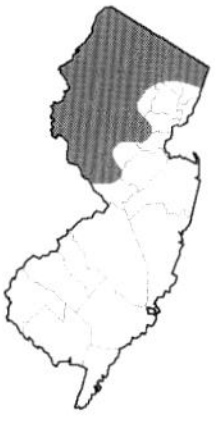

YEAR-ROUND

Size: 19" (48 cm)

Male: Large, crow-sized black-backed woodpecker with bright red crest on head. Long gray bill with red mustache. Leading edge of wings white, flashing brightly when flying.

Female: same as male, but has a black forehead and lacks red mustache

Juvenile: similar to adult, only duller and browner overall

Nest: cavity; male and female excavate; 1 brood per year

Eggs: 3-5; white, unmarked

Incubation: 15-18 days; female and male incubate, female during day, male at night

Fledging: 26-28 days; female and male feed young

Migration: non-migrator

Food: insects, suet, will come to suet feeders

Compare: Red-headed Woodpecker (pg. 33) is about half the size, and has an all-red head, black back and white rump.

Stan's Notes: Our largest woodpecker, it excavates long oval holes up to several feet long in tree trunks, searching for insects. Large chips of wood lay at the base of excavated trees. Will drum on hollow branches, chimneys, etc., to announce its territory. Relatively shy bird that prefers large tracts of woodland. The young are fed regurgitated insects. Favorite food is carpenter ants.

male
female pg. 159

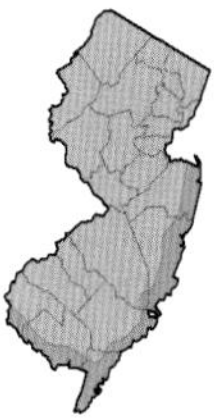

MIGRATION
WINTER

Common Goldeneye
Bucephala clangula

Size: 18½-20" (47-50 cm)

Male: A mostly white duck with a black back, a large, puffy green head and a large white spot in front of each bright golden eye.

Female: brown and gray, a large dark brown head, gray body, white collar, bright golden eyes

Juvenile: same as female

Nest: cavity; female lines former woodpecker cavity; 1 brood per year

Eggs: 8-10; light green without markings

Incubation: 28-32 days; female incubates

Fledging: 56-59 days; female leads young to food

Migration: complete, to southern states

Food: aquatic plants, insects

Compare: Similar to, but larger than, the black and white male Lesser Scaup (pg. 41). Look for distinctive white mark in front of its golden eye and white chest.

Stan's Notes: Known for their loud whistling, which is produced by their wings in flight. In late winter and early spring, males often attract females through elaborate displays, throwing their heads backwards while uttering a single raspy note. Females will lay eggs in other goldeneye nests, resulting in some mothers incubating up to 30 eggs. Received its common name from its obvious bright golden eyes.

soaring

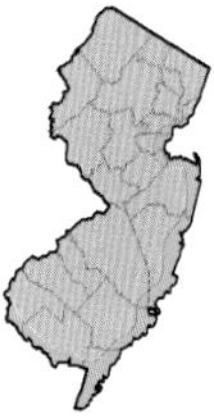

MIGRATION
SUMMER

Osprey
Pandion haliaetus

Size: 24" (60 cm); up to 6-foot wingspan

Male: Large eagle-like bird with white belly and black brown back. Large wings are angled (cocked) backwards with black "wrist" marks. White head with a black streak across eyes.

Female: same as male

Juvenile: same as adult

Nest: platform; female and male build; 1 brood per year

Eggs: 2-4; white with brown markings

Incubation: 32-42 days; female and male incubate

Fledging: 48-58 days; male and female feed young

Migration: complete, to Mexico, Central and South Americas

Food: fish

Compare: Bald Eagle (pg. 59) is on average ten inches larger, and has an all-white head and tail. Immature Bald Eagle is all brown with white speckles. Look for a white belly and dark stripe across eye to identify Osprey.

Stan's Notes: Ospreys are in a family all their own. It is the only raptor that will plunge into the water to catch fish. Look for its angulated wings while in flight. Nests on man-made towers and tall dead trees. Can hover for a few seconds before diving. Carries fish in a head-first position during flight for better aerodynamics. Recent studies show that male and female might mate for life, but don't migrate to the same wintering grounds.

juvenile
breeding

YEAR-ROUND

Great Black-backed Gull
Larus marinus

Size: 30" (76 cm); up to 5½-foot wingspan

Male: Extremely large gull. Breeding plumage of white head, chest and belly. Black back and wings. Distinctive yellow bill with orange mark near the end of lower bill. Pink legs.

Female: same as male

Juvenile: gray and brown, lacking any large black spots, gray bill

Nest: ground; male and female build; 1 brood per year

Eggs: 2-3; olive with sparse brown markings

Incubation: 26-29 days; female and male incubate

Fledging: 49-56 days; male and female feed young

Migration: complete, to East coast and Bermuda

Food: fish, insects, crustaceans

Compare: Larger than the Ring-billed Gull (pg. 267), Herring Gull (pg. 271) and Laughing Gull (pg. 265). Look for white head, black back and bright yellow bill with orange spot.

Stan's Notes: One of the largest gulls, the Great Black-backed Gull is a "four-year" gull, meaning that it goes through four distinct color phases to reach adulthood. Often difficult to distinguish, but depends upon the amount of black on the bird. First year: lacking any black on back, gray bill. Second summer: small amounts of black and a pale yellow bill with black tip. Third summer: much more black on back and wings, yellow bill with black tip. Fourth summer or adult breeding: black back and wings.

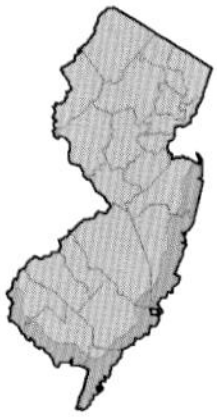

MIGRATION
WINTER

Common Loon
Gavia immer

Size: 28-36" (71-90 cm)

Male: Large, familiar black-and-white bird of the lakes. Checkerboard back with white necklace, black head and deep red eye. Long, pointed black bill in summer. Entirely gray body and bill in fall and winter.

Female: same as male

Juvenile: gray version of adult, without red eye

Nest: platform, on the ground; female and male build; 1 brood per year

Eggs: 2; olive brown, occasionally brown markings

Incubation: 26-31 days; female and male incubate

Fledging: 75-80 days; female and male feed young

Migration: complete, to Gulf coast, southern states and Mexico

Food: fish, aquatic insects

Compare: Double-crested Cormorant (pg. 23) has a yellow bill and black chest.

Stan's Notes: A true symbol of the wildness of our lakes. Prefers clear lakes because it hunts for fish by eyesight. Legs are set so far back that it has a hard time walking on land, but it's a great swimmer. Its name comes from the Swedish word *lom*, meaning "lame," for the awkward way it walks on land. Its unique call suggests the wild laughter of a demented person, and led to the phrase "crazy as a loon." Young ride on the backs of swimming parents. Adults will perform distraction displays to protect young. Very sensitive to disturbance during nesting and will abandon nest.

soaring

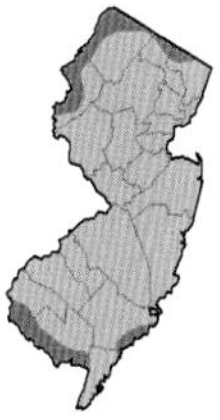

Bald Eagle
Haliaeetus leucocephalus

Size: 31-37" (79-94 cm); up to 7-foot wingspan

Male: Dark brown-to-black body and wings set off by a pure white head and tail. Large, curved yellow bill and yellow feet.

Female: same as male, only slightly larger

Juvenile: dark brown with white spots or speckles throughout its body and wings, gray bill

Nest: massive platform; female and male build; 1 brood per year

Eggs: 2; off-white, unmarked

Incubation: 34-36 days; female and male incubate

Fledging: 75-90 days; female and male feed young

Migration: partial migrator, to southeastern states

Food: fish, carrion, ducks

Compare: Larger than the Turkey Vulture (pg. 21). Mature Bald Eagle has white head and tail. Turkey Vulture has two-toned wings and flies with its wings in a V shape, unlike the straight-out wing position of Eagle.

Stan's Notes: Often seen soaring, this bird is making a comeback in New Jersey. Juveniles attain white head and tail at about 4 to 5 years of age. For their midair mating ritual, one bird flips upside down, locking talons with another. Both tumble until they break apart to continue flying. Bald Eagle returns to the same nest every year, adding sticks, enlarging it to massive proportions, at times up to 1,000 pounds. Thought to mate for life, but will switch mates if not successful reproducing.

Tree Swallow

Tachycineta bicolor

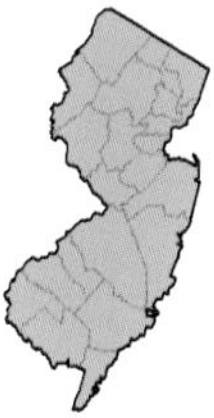

SUMMER

Size: 5-6" (13-15 cm)

Male: Blue green in spring and greener in fall. Appears to change color in direct sunlight. White belly, a notched tail and pointed wing tips.

Female: similar to male, duller

Juvenile: gray brown with white belly and grayish breast band

Nest: cavity; female and male line former woodpecker cavity or nest box; 1 brood per year

Eggs: 4-6; white, unmarked

Incubation: 13-16 days; female incubates

Fledging: 20-24 days; female and male feed young

Migration: complete, to Mexico and Central America

Food: insects

Compare: Similar color to Purple Martin (pg. 69), but smaller and has white chest and belly. Barn Swallow (pg. 65) has rust belly and deeply forked tail.

Stan's Notes: The first swallow to return each spring. Easily attracted to your yard with a nest box. Competes with Eastern Bluebirds for nest boxes. Travels great distances to find dropped feathers to line its grass nest. Sometimes seen playing by chasing after dropped feathers. Often seen flying back and forth across open fields, feeding on insects. Gathers in large flocks to migrate.

female pg. 95
male

Indigo Bunting
Passerina cyanea

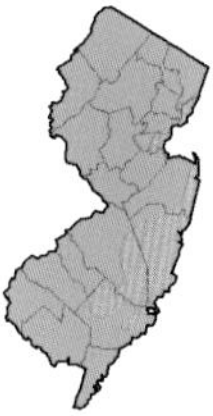

MIGRATION
SUMMER

Size: 5½" (14 cm)

Male: A vibrant blue finch-like bird. Scattered dark markings on wings and tail.

Female: light brown bird with faint markings

Juvenile: similar to female

Nest: cup; female builds; 2 broods per year

Eggs: 3-4; pale blue, unmarked

Incubation: 12-13 days; female incubates

Fledging: 10-11 days; female feeds young

Migration: complete, to Mexico, Central America and South America

Food: insects, seeds, fruit, will visit seed feeders

Compare: Smaller than Eastern Bluebird (pg. 67) and lacking Bluebird's red chest patch.

Stan's Notes: Usually only the males are noticed. Actually a black bird, as it doesn't have any blue pigment in its feathers. As with Blue Jays, the sunlight is refracted within the structure of the bunting's feathers, making them appear blue. Appears iridescent in direct sunlight. Molts to acquire body feathers with gray tips, which quickly wear off to reveal bright blue plumage. Males often sing from treetops to attract mates. Will come to feeders in spring before insects are plentiful. Mostly seen along woodland edges, feeding on insects. Migrates at night in flocks of five to ten birds. A late migrant, with males returning before females and juveniles. Males nearly always return to previous year's nest site. Juveniles move to within a mile from birth site.

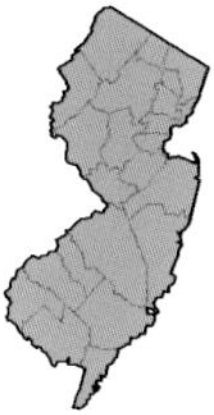

SUMMER

Barn Swallow
Hirundo rustica

Size: 7" (18 cm)

Male: A sleek swallow with a blue black back, cinnamon bell, and reddish brown chin. White spots on long forked tail.

Female: same as male, only slightly duller

Juvenile: similar to adult, with tan belly and chin and shorter tail

Nest: cup; female and male build; 2 broods per year

Eggs: 4-5; white with brown markings

Incubation: 13-17 days; female incubates

Fledging: 18-23 days; female and male feed young

Migration: complete, to South America

Food: insects, prefers beetles, wasps and flies

Compare: Tree Swallow (pg. 61) has white belly and chin, and notched tail. The Chimney Swift (pg. 77) has narrow pointed tail with wings longer than body. Purple Martin (pg. 69) is nearly two inches larger and has a dark purple belly.

Stan's Notes: Of the six swallows in New Jersey, this is the only one with a deeply forked tail. Unlike other swallows, the Barn Swallow rarely glides in flight, so look for continuous flapping. It builds mud nests using up to 1,000 beak-loads of mud, often in or on barns. Nests in colonies of four to six, but nesting alone is not uncommon. They drink while flying by skimming water or getting water from wet leaves. They also bathe while flying through rain or sprinklers.

male

female

EASTERN BLUEBIRD
Sialia sialis

YEAR-ROUND

Size: 7" (18 cm)

Male: Reminiscent of its larger cousin, American Robin, with a rusty red breast and white belly. Sky blue head, back and tail.

Female: shares rusty red breast and white belly, but is grayer with faint blue tail and wings

Juvenile: similar to female, with spots on chest, blue wing markings

Nest: cavity, old woodpecker cavity or man-made nest box; female builds; 2 broods per year

Eggs: 4-5; pale blue, unmarked

Incubation: 12-14 days; female incubates

Fledging: 15-18 days; male and female feed young

Migration: complete, to southern states

Food: insects, fruit

Compare: Male Indigo Bunting (pg. 63) is nearly all blue, lacking rusty red chest. The Blue Jay (pg. 71) is considerably larger with a crest and white markings.

Stan's Notes: Once nearly eliminated from New Jersey due to a lack of nesting cavities, bluebirds have made a remarkable comeback with the aid of bird enthusiasts who have put up thousands of bluebird boxes. Easily tamed, they will come to a shallow dish with mealworms in it. Perches on tree or fence post and waits for grasshoppers. Young of first brood will help raise young of second. Gathers in large family groups to migrate. Males return first in spring, followed by females a week or two later.

male

female

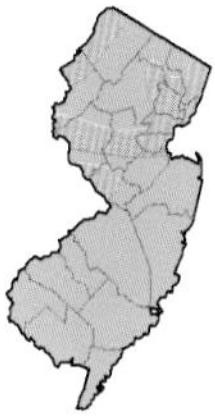

MIGRATION
SUMMER

Purple Martin
Progne subis

Size: 8½" (22 cm)

Male: A large swallow-shaped bird with purple head, back and belly. Black wings and tail. Notched tail.

Female: gray purple head and back with a whitish belly, darker wings and tail

Juvenile: same as female

Nest: cavity; female and male line cavity of house; 1 brood per year

Eggs: 4-5; white, unmarked

Incubation: 15-18 days; female incubates

Fledging: 26-30 days; male and female feed young

Migration: complete, to South America

Food: insects

Compare: The male is the only dark-purple-bellied swallow. Usually only seen in groups.

Stan's Notes: The largest swallows in North America. Formerly nested in tree cavities, but now nearly exclusively nest in man-made nest boxes in New Jersey. Their main diet consists of dragonflies, not mosquitoes as once thought. Often drink and bathe while flying by skimming water or flying through rain. Return to same nest site each year. Males arrive before females and yearlings. Often nest within 100 feet of a human dwelling, and in fact, the most successful colonies are located within this distance. Young strike out to form new colonies. Huge colonies gather in autumn to migrate to South America.

YEAR-ROUND

Blue Jay
Cyanocitta cristata

Size: 12" (30 cm)

Male: A large bright light blue and white bird with a black necklace. Crest on head moves up and down at will. Gray belly with white face. White wing bars on blue wing. Blue tail with black spots and white tip.

Female: same as male

Juvenile: same as adult, only duller

Nest: cup; female and male build; 1-2 broods per year

Eggs: 4-5; green to blue with brown markings

Incubation: 16-18 days; female incubates

Fledging: 17-21 days; female and male feed young

Migration: non-migrator to partial migrator, moves around to find abundant food source

Food: insects, fruit, carrion, seeds, nuts, attracted to seed feeders

Compare: Eastern Bluebird (pg. 67) is much smaller and lacks the crest. The Belted Kingfisher (pg. 73) lacks vivid blue color and black necklace of the Blue Jay.

Stan's Notes: One of the few birds to cache food. Will scream like a hawk to scatter birds at a feeder before approaching. Feathers don't have blue pigment; refracted sunlight casts blue light. Known as the alarm of the forest, screaming at any intruders in the woods. Is known to eat eggs or young birds from the nests of other birds.

male

female

YEAR-ROUND

Belted Kingfisher

Ceryle alcyon

Size: 13" (33 cm)

Male: Large blue gray bird with white belly. Broad blue gray breast band and a ragged crest that can be raised and lowered at will. Large head with long thick black bill. Small white spot directly in front of red brown eye. Wing tips black with splashes of white that flash when flying.

Female: same as male, but has an additional rusty breast band and flank

Juvenile: same as adult

Nest: cavity; female and male excavate; 1 brood per year

Eggs: 6-7; white, unmarked

Incubation: 23-24 days; female and male incubate

Fledging: 23-24 days; female and male feed young

Migration: complete, to southern states, Central and South Americas

Food: small fish

Compare: Similar in size to the Blue Jay (pg. 71), but Kingfisher is darker blue with larger, more ragged crest.

Stan's Notes: Seen perched on branches near water, it dives head-first for small fish and returns to a branch to eat. Has a loud machine-gun-like call. Excavates a deep cavity in bank of river or lake. Parents drop dead fish into water, teaching young to dive. Regurgitates pellets of bone after meals, being unable to pass bones through digestive tract. Mates recognize each other by call.

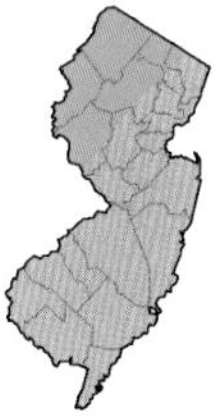

MIGRATION
SUMMER

CHESTNUT-SIDED WARBLER
Dendroica pensylvanica

Size: 5" (13 cm)

Male: A colorful combination of a yellow cap and black mask set against a white face, chin, chest and belly. Two yellow wing bars. Chestnut-colored flanks. Gray wings.

Female: similar to male, but flanks duller brown

Juvenile: similar to female, lime green head and back, white eye ring and bright yellow wing bars, lacks chestnut sides

Nest: cup; female builds; 1 brood per year

Eggs: 3-5; white with brown markings

Incubation: 12-13 days; female incubates

Fledging: 10-12 days; female and male feed young

Migration: complete, to Central America

Food: insects, berries

Compare: Shares yellow cap with the Yellow-rumped Warbler (pg. 189), but lacks yellow sides and rump. The Yellow Warbler (pg. 289) is nearly all yellow and lacks the Chestnut's white chest and chestnut-colored flanks.

Stan's Notes: Prefers young, open aspen forest. Look for this attractive warbler in the spring, hopping high in the branches while it hunts for insects. You will usually only get a glimpse of this fast-moving warbler. Will hold its tail in an uplifted position, showing white tail. Not uncommon for this bird to approach humans in defense of a nest site.

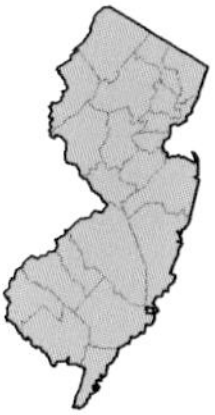

SUMMER

CHIMNEY SWIFT
Chaetura pelagica

Size: 5" (13 cm)

Male: A nondescript, all-brown swallow-shaped bird, usually only seen flying. Long thin body with pointed tail and head. Long swept-back wings are longer than body.

Female: same as male

Juvenile: same as adult

Nest: half cup; female and male build; 1 brood per year

Eggs: 4-5; white, unmarked

Incubation: 19-21 days; female and male incubate

Fledging: 28-30 days; female and male feed young

Migration: complete, to South America

Food: insects

Compare: Considerably smaller than Purple Martin (pg. 69) and lacks Martin's iridescent purple color. Barn Swallow (pg. 65) has forked tail, compared with the pointed tail of the Chimney Swift. Tree Swallow (pg. 61) has white belly and blue green back.

Stan's Notes: Often called Flying Cigar due to its pointed body shape. Spends all day flying, rarely perching. They bathe and drink by skimming across water surfaces. Hundreds nest and roost in large chimneys, hence the common name. One of the fastest flyers in the bird world. Unique in-flight twittering call is often heard before bird is seen. Fly in groups, feeding on flying insects nearly 100 feet in the air. Nest, made of tiny twigs, is cemented with saliva and attached to inside of chimneys or hollow trees.

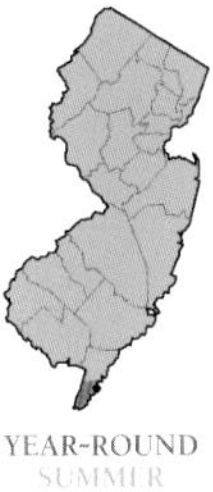

Chipping Sparrow

Spizella passerina

Size: 5" (13 cm)

Male: A small gray brown sparrow with a clear gray chest, rusty crown, white eyebrow with a black eye line, a thin gray black bill and two faint wing bars.

Female: same as male

Juvenile: similar to adult, but has streaked chest and lacks rusty cap

Nest: cup; female builds; 2 broods per year

Eggs: 3-5; blue green with brown markings

Incubation: 11-14 days; female incubates

Fledging: 10-12 days; female and male feed young

Migration: complete, to southern states, Central America and Mexico

Food: insects, seeds, will come to ground feeders

Compare: Similar to American Tree Sparrow (pg. 99), which shares the rusty crown, but lacks the dark eye stripe. Look for clear gray chest of Chipping Sparrow. Two inches smaller than the rusty Fox Sparrow (pg. 107).

Stan's Notes: Common garden or yard bird often seen feeding below feeders on dropped seeds. Gathers in large family groups to feed each autumn in preparation for migration. Nest is placed low in dense shrubs and is almost always lined with animal hair. Often just called Chippy. Received its common name from the male's slow "chip" call. Migrates at night in flocks of 20 to 30 birds.

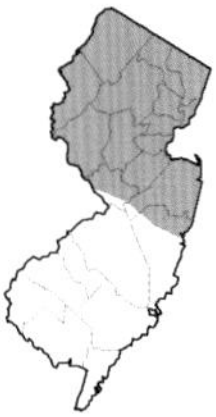

WINTER

Common Redpoll
Carduelis flammea

Size: 5" (13 cm)

Male: A small sparrow-like bird with a bright red crown and black spot under chin. Heavily streaked back and a splash of raspberry red on chest.

Female: same as male, only without the raspberry red on chest

Juvenile: browner than adult, lacking red cap and with dark streaks on chest

Nest: cup; female builds; 1 brood per year, occasionally 2

Eggs: 4-5; pale green with purple markings

Incubation: 10-11 days; female incubates

Fledging: 11-12 days; female and male feed young

Migration: irruptive, moves into New Jersey from Canada for some winters

Food: seeds, insects, will come to seed feeders

Compare: Slightly smaller than the male Purple Finch (pg. 253), it lacks the male Purple Finch's red back and rump. Similar to the male House Finch (pg. 251), the Redpoll lacks red rump. Note Redpoll's black spot under bill and bright red cap.

Stan's Notes: Name is derived from the color and "taking a poll" or counting heads. Winters in New Jersey after summering in the far reaches of Canada. Winter flocks of up to 100 birds are not uncommon. Bathes in open water or snow in winter. Much like the Black-capped Chickadee, it can be tamed and hand fed.

male pg. 251
female

House Finch
Carpodacus mexicanus

YEAR-ROUND

Size: 5" (13 cm)

Female: A plain brown bird with a heavily streaked white chest.

Male: orange red face, chest and rump, with a dark brown marking behind eye, brown wings streaked with white, white belly with brown streaks, brown cap

Juvenile: similar to female

Nest: cup, sometimes in cavities; female builds; 2 broods per year

Eggs: 4-5; pale blue, lightly marked

Incubation: 12-14 days; female incubates

Fledging: 15-19 days; female and male feed young

Migration: non-migrator to partial migrator, moves around to find food

Food: seeds, fruit, leaf buds, will come to seed feeders

Compare: Very similar to female Purple Finch (pg. 97). Lacking Purple Finch's bold white eyebrow. The female American Goldfinch (pg. 283) has a clear chest and white wing bars. Very similar to Pine Siskin (pg. 87), but without Siskin's yellow wing bars.

Stan's Notes: The House Finch was originally introduced to Long Island, New York, in the 1940s from western America. A very social bird, it visits feeders in small flocks. Seems to prefer nesting in hanging flower baskets. Incubating female is fed by male. Loud and cheerful warbling song.

House Wren
Troglodytes aedon

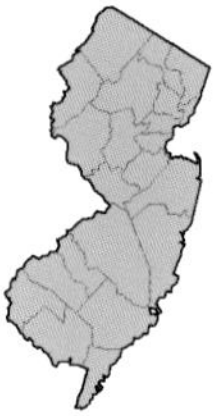

SUMMER

Size: 5" (13 cm)

Male: A small all-brown bird with light brown marking on tail and wings. Brown, slightly curved bill. Often holds its tail erect.

Female: same as male

Juvenile: same as adult

Nest: cavity; female and male line just about any cavity; 2 broods per year

Eggs: 4-6; tan with brown markings

Incubation: 10-13 days; female and male incubate

Fledging: 12-15 days; female and male feed young

Migration: complete, to southern states and Mexico

Food: insects

Compare: Distinguished from Carolina Wren (pg. 89) by the lack of brow marking.

Stan's Notes: Prolific songsters, they sing from dawn to dusk during mating season. Easily attracted to nesting boxes. In spring, the male chooses several prospective nesting cavities and places a few small twigs in each. Female inspects each, chooses one, and finishes the nest building. She will completely fill nest cavity with uniformly small twigs, then line a small depression at back of cavity with pine needles and grass. Often has trouble fitting long twigs through nest cavity hole. Tries many different directions and approaches until successful.

YEAR-ROUND
WINTER

PINE SISKIN
Carduelis pinus

Size: 5" (13 cm)

Male: A small brown finch with heavily streaked back, breast and belly. Yellow wing bars and yellow at base of tail. Thin bill.

Female: same as male

Juvenile: similar to adult, with light yellow tinge throughout chest and chin

Nest: modified cup; female builds; 2 broods per year

Eggs: 3-4; greenish blue with brown markings

Incubation: 12-13 days; female incubates

Fledging: 14-15 days; female and male feed young

Migration: irruptive, moves around the state to find food

Food: seeds, insects, will come to seed feeders

Compare: Female American Goldfinch (pg. 283) lacks streaks and has white wing bars. Female House Finch (pg. 83) has streaked chest, but lacks yellow wing bars. Female Purple Finch (pg. 97) has bold white eyebrow.

Stan's Notes: Usually considered a winter finch. Seen in flocks of less than 20 and are often associated with Evening Grosbeaks. Can be found throughout the state in heavy invasion years, but is absent in some winters. Will come to thistle feeders. Travels and breeds in small groups with nests often only a few feet apart. Males feed females during incubation. Juveniles lose yellow tint of chest and chin by late summer of first year.

YEAR-ROUND

Carolina Wren
Thryothorus ludovicianus

Size: 5½" (14 cm)

Male: Warm rusty brown head and back with an orange yellow chest and belly. White throat and a prominent white eye stripe. Short stubby tail often cocked up.

Female: same as male

Juvenile: same as adult

Nest: cavity; female and male build; 2 broods per year, sometimes 3

Eggs: 4-6; white, sometimes pink or creamy, with brown markings

Incubation: 12-14 days; female incubates

Fledging: 12-14 days; female and male feed young

Migration: non-migrator

Food: insects, fruit, few seeds

Compare: Similar to the House Wren (pg. 85), but the Carolina Wren has the prominent white eyebrow. Look for the stubby upturned tail.

Stan's Notes: Mates are long-term, remaining together throughout the year in permanent territories. Will sing throughout the year. The male is known to sing up to 40 different song types, singing one song repeatedly before switching to another. Females also sing, resulting in duets. Male often takes over feeding first brood of young while the female renests. Range expands northward in years with mild winters. Will nest in birdhouses or in the most unusual places, such as mailboxes, bumpers of cars, broken taillights or just about any other cavity. Found in woodland or brushy yards.

Song Sparrow
Melospiza melodia

YEAR-ROUND

Size: 5-6" (13-15 cm)

Male: Common brown sparrow with heavy dark streaks on chest coalescing into a central dark spot.

Female: same as male

Juvenile: similar to adult, finely streaked chest without central spot

Nest: cup; female builds; 2 broods per year

Eggs: 3-4; pale blue to green with reddish brown marks

Incubation: 12-14 days; female incubates

Fledging: 9-12 days; female and male feed young

Migration: complete, to southern states

Food: insects, seeds, rarely visits seed feeders

Compare: Similar to other brown sparrows, look for heavily streaked chest with central dark spot.

Stan's Notes: Many Song Sparrow subspecies or varieties, but central dark spot carries through each variant. While the female builds another nest for second brood, the male often takes over feeding the young. Returns to similar area each year, defending its small territory by singing from thick shrubs. Common host of Brown-headed Cowbird. Ground feeders, look for them to scratch simultaneously with both feet to expose seeds. Unlike many sparrow species, Song Sparrows rarely flock together.

male pg. 191
female

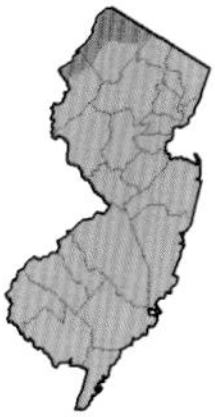

YEAR-ROUND
WINTER

Dark-eyed Junco
Junco hyemalis

Size: 5½" (14 cm)

Female: A round bird with a tan-to-brown chest, head and back. White belly, ivory-to-pink bill and dark eye. Since the outermost tail feathers are white, tail appears as a white V in flight.

Male: same as female, only slate gray to charcoal

Juvenile: similar to female, with streaked chest and head

Nest: cup; female and male build; 2 broods per year

Eggs: 3-5; white with reddish brown markings

Incubation: 12-13 days; female incubates

Fledging: 10-13 days; male and female feed young

Migration: complete, all across United States

Food: seeds, insects, will come to seed feeders

Compare: Rarely confused with other birds. Large flocks come to feed under bird feeders.

Stan's Notes: One of New Jersey's most common winter birds. Usually seen on the ground in small flocks. Migrates from Canada to New Jersey and beyond. Small population stays year-round in northern New Jersey. Males tend to migrate farther south than females. Look for white outer tail feathers that flash in flight. Several species of juncos have now been combined into one, simply called Dark-eyed Junco. Most comfortable on the ground, juncos "double-scratch" with both feet to expose seeds and insects. Consume many weed seeds. A flocking bird, it adheres to a rigid social hierarchy with dominant birds chasing less dominant birds.

female
male pg.63

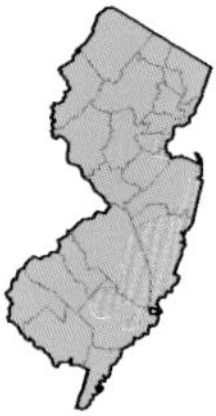

MIGRATION
SUMMER

Indigo Bunting
Passerina cyanea

Size: 5½" (14 cm)

Female: A light brown finch-like bird with faint streaking on light tan chest. Wings have very faint blue cast with indistinct wing bars.

Male: vibrant blue finch-like bird, scattered dark markings on wings and tail

Juvenile: similar to female

Nest: cup; female builds; 2 broods per year

Eggs: 3-4; pale blue, unmarked

Incubation: 12-13 days; female incubates

Fledging: 10-11 days; female feeds young

Migration: complete, to Mexico, Central America and South America

Food: insects, seeds, fruit, will visit seed feeders

Compare: Similar to female finches. The female American Goldfinch (pg. 283) has white wing bars. Female Purple Finch (pg. 97) has a heavily streaked chest and white eye lines. Female House Finch (pg. 83) also has heavily streaked chest.

Stan's Notes: A secretive bird, usually only the males are seen. Males often sing from treetops to attract mates. Will come to feeders in spring before insects are plentiful. Mostly seen along woodland edges, feeding on insects. Migrates at night in flocks of five to ten birds. A late migrant, with males returning before females and juveniles. Juveniles move to within a mile from birth site.

male pg. 253
female

Purple Finch
Carpodacus purpureus

Size: 6" (15 cm)

Female: A plain brown bird with a heavily streaked chest. Prominent white eye line.

Male: raspberry red head, cap, breast, back and rump, brownish wings and tail

Juvenile: same as female

Nest: cup; female and male build; 1 brood per year

Eggs: 4-5; greenish blue with brown markings

Incubation: 12-13 days; female incubates

Fledging: 13-14 days; female and male feed young

Migration: irruptive, moves around the state to find food

Food: seeds, insects, fruit, will come to seed feeders

Compare: The female House Finch (pg. 83) lacks white eyebrow. The Pine Siskin (pg. 87) has yellow wing bars. The female American Goldfinch (pg. 283) has a clear chest and white wing bars.

Stan's Notes: Year-round resident of northern New Jersey. Travels in flocks of up to 50. Comes to seed feeders along with House Finches, making it hard to tell them apart. A rich loud song and a distinctive "tic" note is made only in flight. Not a purple color, the Latin name *purpureus* means "crimson" or other reddish color.

side view

front view

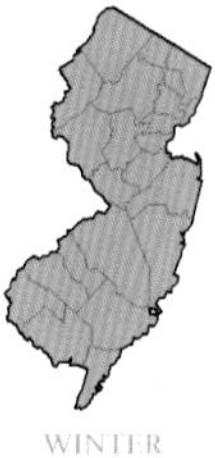

AMERICAN TREE SPARROW
Spizella arborea

Size: 6" (15 cm)

Male: A common brown sparrow with tan breast and rusty crown. Note single black spot in center of breast. Upper bill dark, lower bill yellow. Two white wing bars. Gray eyebrow.

Female: same as male

Juvenile: lacking rusty crown, has a streaked chest often obscuring the central dark spot

Nest: cup; female builds; 1 brood per year

Eggs: 3-5; green white with brown markings

Incubation: 12-13 days; female incubates

Fledging: 8-10 days; female and male feed young

Migration: complete, throughout North America

Food: insects, seeds, occasionally comes to feeders

Compare: Looks similar to other sparrows, so look closely for the single dark spot in the center of the breast. Shares a rusty crown with the Chipping Sparrow (pg. 79), but lacks Chippy's distinctive white eyebrow and black eye line. Song Sparrow (pg. 91) has a heavily streaked chest.

Stan's Notes: A regular winter bird feeder visitor throughout the state. Also seen during spring and fall migrations in small flocks of 2 to 200. Sometimes called Winter Chippy, since it looks similar to the Chipping Sparrow, a summer visitor and year-round southern resident. Nests in northern Canada.

male

female

House Sparrow
Passer domesticus

YEAR-ROUND

Size: 6" (15 cm)

Male: Medium sparrow-like bird with large black spot on chin extending down to the chest. Brown back with white wing bar. A gray belly and crown.

Female: all-light-brown bird, lacking black throat patch and wing bar, slightly smaller

Juvenile: similar to female

Nest: domed cup nest, within cavity; female and male build; 2-3 broods per year

Eggs: 4-6; white with brown markings

Incubation: 10-12 days; female incubates

Fledging: 14-17 days; female and male feed young

Migration: non-migrator, moves around to find food

Food: seeds, insects, fruit, comes to seed feeders

Compare: Lacks the rusty crown of American Tree Sparrow (pg. 99) and Chipping Sparrow (pg. 79). Look for male House Sparrow's black bib. Female has clear chest and no marking on head (cap).

Stan's Notes: Introduced from Europe to Central Park, New York, in 1850 and now found throughout North America. These birds are not really sparrows, but members of the Weaver Finch family, characterized by large, oversized domed nests. Constructs a nest containing scraps of plastic, paper and whatever else is available. Aggressive bird that will kill the young of other birds in order to take over a cavity. Familiar city bird, nearly always in flocks.

white-
striped

tan-
striped

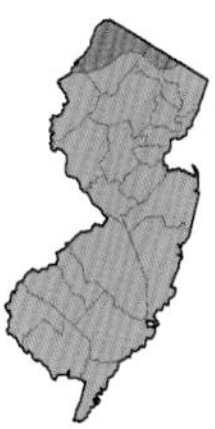

YEAR-ROUND
WINTER

White-throated Sparrow
Zonotrichia albicollis

Size: 6-7" (15-18 cm)

Male: A brown sparrow with gray tan chest and belly. Small yellow spot between the eyes, called lore. Distinctive white throat patch. Crown has white or tan stripes alternating with black stripes.

Female: same as male

Juvenile: brown version of adult, eyebrow and throat gray with heavily streaked chest

Nest: cup; female builds; 1 brood per year

Eggs: 4-6; varies between greenish, bluish and creamy white, with red brown markings

Incubation: 11-14 days; female incubates

Fledging: 10-12 days; female and male feed young

Migration: complete, to southern states and Mexico

Food: insects, fruit, seeds, will come to ground feeders

Compare: The White-crowned Sparrow (pg. 105) has a black-and-white striped crown, without the yellow lore or white throat patch.

Stan's Notes: There are two color variations (polymorphic) of White-throated Sparrows: tan-striped and white-striped. Studies indicate the white-striped adults tend to mate with the tan-striped birds. No indication why. Nests are built on the ground under small trees in bogs and coniferous forests.

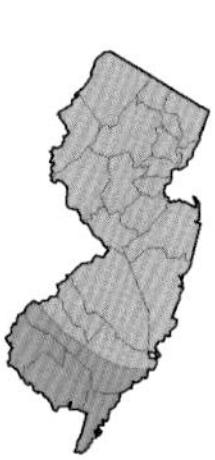

MIGRATION
WINTER

White-crowned Sparrow
Zonotrichia leucophrys

Size: 6½-7½" (16-19 cm)

Male: A brown sparrow with gray chest and a black-and-white striped crown. Small thin pink bill.

Female: same as male

Juvenile: similar to adult, with brown stripes on head instead of white

Nest: cup; female builds; 2 broods per year

Eggs: 3-5; varies between greenish, bluish and whitish, with red brown markings

Incubation: 11-14 days; female incubates

Fledging: 8-12 days; male and female feed young

Migration: complete, to southern states and Mexico

Food: insects, seeds, berries, will come to ground feeders

Compare: The White-throated Sparrow (pg. 103) has white- or tan-striped crown, white throat patch, and yellow spot between eyes and bill, with a blackish bill.

Stan's Notes: Doesn't nest in New Jersey. Males take most of the responsibility of raising young while female starts a second brood. Only 9 to 12 days separate the broods. Feeds on the ground by scratching backwards with both feet at the same time. Usually seen in groups of up to 20 during spring and fall migrations.

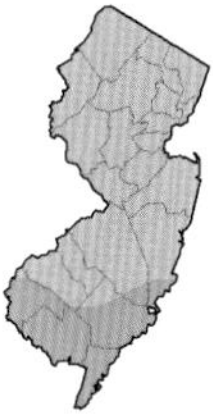

MIGRATION
WINTER

Fox Sparrow
Passerella iliaca

Size: 7" (18 cm)

Male: A plump rusty-red sparrow with a heavily streaked, rust-colored breast and solid rust tail. Head and back are mottled with gray.

Female: same as male

Juvenile: same as adult

Nest: cup; female builds; 2 broods per year

Eggs: 2-4; pale green with reddish markings

Incubation: 12-14 days; female incubates

Fledging: 10-11 days; female and male feed young

Migration: complete, to southern states

Food: insects, seeds, comes to feeders

Compare: Similar coloration as the Brown Thrasher (pg. 131), but the Fox Sparrow is smaller, plumper and has a smaller bill. Rusty color differentiates it from all other sparrows.

Stan's Notes: One of the largest sparrows, it is often only seen under seed feeders during spring and autumn migrations. Scratches like a chicken with both feet at the same time to find seeds and insects. Nests on the ground in brush and forest edges in Canada. The name "Sparrow" comes from the Anglo-Saxon word *spearwa*, which means "flutterer," as applied to any small bird. "Fox" refers to the bird's rusty color.

male pg. 3
female

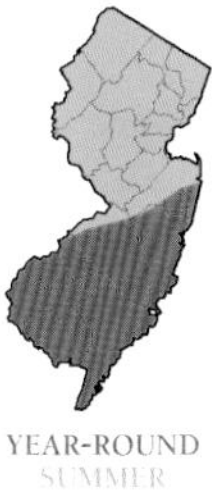

EASTERN TOWHEE
Pipilo erythrophthalmus

Size: 7-8" (18-20 cm)

Female: A mostly light brown bird with rusty red brown sides and white belly. Long brown tail with white tip. Short, stout, pointed bill with rich red eye. White wing patches flash in flight.

Male: similar to female, but is black, not brown

Juvenile: light brown, heavily streaked head, chest and belly, long dark tail with white tip

Nest: cup; female builds; 2 broods per year

Eggs: 3-4; creamy white with brown markings

Incubation: 12-13 days; female incubates

Fledging: 10-12 days; female and male feed young

Migration: complete, to southern states and South America

Food: insects, seeds, fruit, comes to ground feeder

Compare: Slightly smaller than the American Robin (pg. 215). Female Rose-breasted Grosbeak (pg. 115) has a heavily streaked chest and white eye mark.

Stan's Notes: Common name comes from its distinctive "tow-hee" call given by both sexes. Mostly known for its characteristic call that sounds like "Drink-your-tea!" White-eyed form in southern states. Seen hopping backward with both feet to rake up leaf litter, called bilateral scratching, in search of insects and seeds. Female broods, but male does most of the feeding of young.

Cedar Waxwing
Bombycilla cedrorum

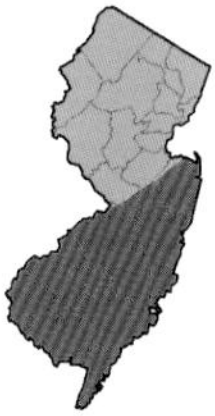

YEAR-ROUND
SUMMER

Size: 7½" (19 cm)

Male: A very sleek-looking brown gray bird with a pointed crest on head, light yellow belly and bandit-like black mask. The tip of its tail is bright yellow and the tips of its wings look as if they have been dipped in red wax.

Female: same as male

Juvenile: slightly smaller, lacking the red wing tips, black mask or sleek appearance, heavily streaked chest

Nest: cup; female and male build; 1 brood per year, occasionally 2

Eggs: 4-6; pale blue with brown markings

Incubation: 10-12 days; female incubates

Fledging: 14-18 days; female and male feed young

Migration: partial migrator

Food: fruit, insects

Compare: Nearly identical to its larger, less common cousin, the Bohemian Waxwing.

Stan's Notes: The name is derived from their red wax-like wing tips and preference for eating small blueberry-like cones of the cedar. Mostly seen in flocks, moving from area to area, looking for berries. More often seen in winter only because naked branches reveal their presence. Spends most of its time at the tops of tall trees. In summer, before berries are abundant, they feed on insects. Listen for the very high-pitched whistling sounds that the birds constantly make. Wanders in winter to find available food supplies.

male pg. 5
female

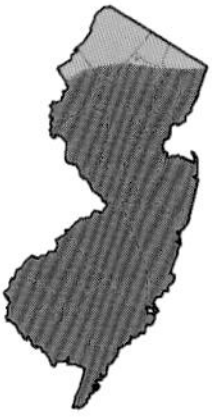

YEAR-ROUND
SUMMER

BROWN-HEADED COWBIRD
Molothrus ater

Size: 7½" (19 cm)

Female: Dull brown gray bird without any obvious markings. Pointed, sharp gray bill.

Male: glossy black bird with chocolate brown head

Juvenile: similar to female, only duller gray with streaked chest

Nest: no nest; lays eggs in nests of other birds

Eggs: 5-7; white with brown markings

Incubation: 10-13 days; host bird incubates eggs

Fledging: 10-11 days; host birds feed young

Migration: complete, to southern states

Food: insects, seeds, will come to seed feeders

Compare: In the blackbird family. The slightly larger female Red-winged Blackbird (pg. 125) has a white eye line and a streaked chest. The European Starling (pg. 7) has speckles, a long, pointed yellow bill and short tail.

Stan's Notes: Of about 750 species of parasitic birds worldwide, this is the only parasitic bird in New Jersey, laying all eggs in host birds' nests, leaving others to raise its young. Cowbirds are known to have laid eggs in nests of over 200 species of birds. Some birds reject cowbird eggs, but most raise them, even to the exclusion of their own young. Look for warblers and other birds feeding young birds twice their own size. At one time they followed bison to feed on the insects attracted to the animals.

female
male pg. 29

ROSE-BREASTED GROSBEAK
Pheucticus ludovicianus

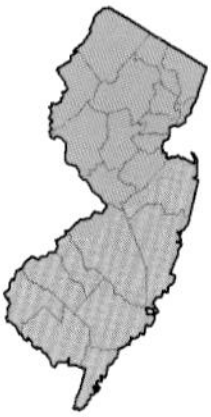

MIGRATION
SUMMER

Size: 7-8" (18-20 cm)

Female: Plump, heavily streaked brown and white bird with obvious white eyebrow line. Wing linings are orange yellow.

Male: plump black-and-white bird with large, triangular rose patch on center of chest, wing linings are rosy red, large ivory bill

Juvenile: same as female

Nest: cup; female and male build; 1-2 broods per year

Eggs: 3-5; blue green with brown markings

Incubation: 13-14 days; female and male incubate

Fledging: 9-12 days; female and male feed young

Migration: complete, to Mexico, Central and South Americas

Food: insects, seeds, fruit, comes to seed feeders

Compare: Females look like large sparrows. Female is larger and has more distinctive eyebrow mark than female Purple Finch (pg. 97). Female House Finch (pg. 83) has no eyebrow mark. Males are very distinctive with no look-alikes.

Stan's Notes: Both females and males sing, but males sing much louder and clearer. Rich robin-like song. White wing patches flash when in flight. The name "Grosbeak" refers to its large bill, used to crush seeds. Male's red breast patch varies in size and shape in each individual. Males arrive first in spring, joined by females several days later. Late to arrive in spring and early to leave in autumn.

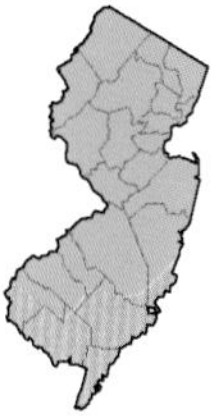

MIGRATION
SUMMER

Spotted Sandpiper
Actitis macularia

Size: 8" (20 cm)

Male: Olive brown back and a white chest with black spots. White line over eye and long bill with long dull yellow legs. Lacks breast spots in fall and winter.

Female: same as male

Juvenile: similar to adult, lacking spots on chest and darker bill

Nest: ground; female and male build; 2 broods per year

Eggs: 3-4; brownish with brown markings

Incubation: 20-24 days; male incubates

Fledging: 17-21 days; male feeds young

Migration: complete, southern states and South America

Food: aquatic insects

Compare: Much smaller than the Greater Yellowlegs (pg. 143) and Lesser Yellowlegs (pg. 129). Look for Spotted Sandpiper's black spots extending from chest down to abdomen.

Stan's Notes: One of the more common sandpipers, females mate with multiple males and lay eggs in up to five different nests. Males incubate and care for young. Constantly bobs tail while standing and walks as if delicately balanced. Flies with wings held in cup-like arc, never really lifted above a horizontal plane. Able to fly straight up out of the water. One of the few shorebirds that will actually dive underwater if pursued. When this bird is in winter plumage, it lacks spots.

winter pg. 205
breeding

Sanderling
Calidris alba

WINTER

Size: 8" (20 cm)

Male: Black legs and bill. During breeding season April to August), head, chest and back are rusty with a white belly. Winter plumage of gray head and back, white belly and a white wing stripe shown only in flight. During the winter, it's the lightest-colored sandpiper on the beach.

Female: same as male

Juvenile: spotty black on head and back, with white belly, black legs and bill

Nest: ground; 1-2 broods per year

Eggs: 3-4; greenish-olive with brown markings

Incubation: 24-30 days; male and female incubate

Fledging: 16-17 days; female and male feed young

Migration: partial to complete, to East and Gulf coasts, South America and West Indies

Food: insects

Compare: Same size as the breeding plumage Spotted Sandpiper (pg. 117), but lacks chest spots.

Stan's Notes: One of the most common shorebirds in New Jersey. Can be seen in groups on sandy beaches, running out with each retreating wave to feed. Occasionally the female mates with several males (polyandry), resulting in males and the female incubating separate nests. Both sexes perform a distraction display if threatened. Nests in the Arctic tundra. Look for a flash of white on the wings when in flight. Declining in populations. Surveys show a more than 80 percent decline in numbers since the 1970s.

winter
pg. 207
breeding

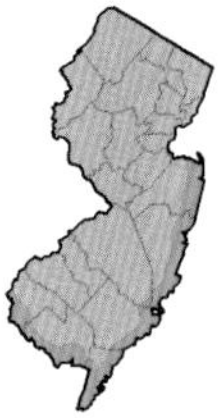

Dunlin
Calidris alpina

Size: 8-9" (20-22.5 cm)

Male: Black legs. Stout bill curved slightly downward at tip. Distinctive breeding plumage of rusty red back with a finely streaked chest and an obvious black patch on belly. Winter plumage of grayish brown back with light gray chest and white belly.

Female: slightly larger than male, with longer bill

Juvenile: slightly rusty back with spotty chest

Nest: ground; male and female build; 1 brood per year

Eggs: 2-4; olive-buff or blue-green with red-brown markings

Incubation: 21-22 days; male and female incubate, male during day, female at night

Fledging: 19-21 days; male feeds young, female often leaves before young fledge

Migration: complete, to the southern coastal states and East, Gulf and Central America coasts

Food: insects

Compare: Similar in size to the breeding Sanderling (pg. 119), look for the obvious black belly patch and curved bill of Dunlin.

Stan's Notes: Flights include heights of 100 feet with brief gliding alternating with shallow flutters, and rhythmic, repeating song. Males tend to fly farther south than females in winter. Huge flocks fly synchronously, twisting and turning, flashing their light and dark undersides.

male pg. 257
female

YEAR-ROUND

NORTHERN CARDINAL
Cardinalis cardinalis

Size: 8-9" (20-22.5 cm)

Female: Buff brown bird with tinges of red on crest and wings, a black mask and large red bill.

Male: red bird with a black mask extending from face down to chin and throat, large red bill and crest

Juvenile: same as female, with blackish gray bill

Nest: cup; female builds; 2-3 broods per year

Eggs: 3-4; bluish white with brown markings

Incubation: 12-13 days; female and male incubate

Fledging: 9-10 days; female and male feed young

Migration: non-migrator

Food: seeds, insects, fruit, will come to seed feeders

Compare: Female Cardinal appears similar to immature cardinal. Look for female's bright red bill.

Stan's Notes: A familiar backyard bird. Look for male feeding female during courtship. Male feeds young of first brood by himself while female builds second nest. Their name comes from the Latin word *cardinalis*, which means "important." Very territorial during spring, it will fight its own reflection in a window. Non-territorial in winter, they gather in small flocks of up to 20 birds. Both male and female sing, and can be heard anytime of year. Listen for their "whata-cheer-cheer-cheer" territorial call in spring.

female
male pg. 9

Red-winged Blackbird
Agelaius phoeniceus

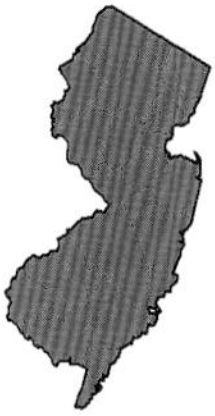

YEAR-ROUND

Size: 8½" (22 cm)

Female: A heavily streaked brown bird with white eyebrow and pointed brown bill.

Male: jet black bird with red and yellow patch on upper wing, pointed black bill

Juvenile: same as female

Nest: cup; female builds; 2-3 broods per year

Eggs: 3-4; bluish green with brown markings

Incubation: 10-12 days; female incubates

Fledging: 11-14 days; female and male feed young

Migration: complete, to southern states, Mexico and Central America

Food: insects, seeds, will come to seed feeders

Compare: Slightly larger than female Brown-headed Cowbird (pg. 113), which lacks white eyebrow and streaks on chest. Similar to the female Rose-breasted Grosbeak (pg. 115), only thinner body and long pointed bill.

Stan's Notes: It is a sure sign of spring when the Red-winged Blackbirds return to the marsh. Flocks of up to 100,000 birds have been reported. Males return before females and defend territories. Will repeat call from top of cattail while showing off red and yellow wing bars, called epaulets. Females choose mate. Nests are usually over shallow water in thick stand of cattails. One of the most widespread and numerous birds in New Jersey. Feeds mostly on seeds in spring and fall, switching to insects during summer.

in flight

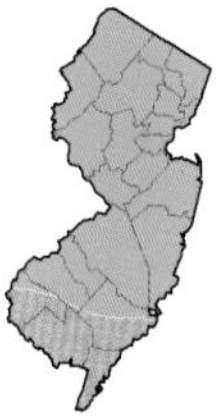

MIGRATION
SUMMER

Common Nighthawk
Chordeiles minor

Size: 9" (22.5 cm)

Male: A camouflaged brown and white bird with white chin. Distinctive white bands across wings and tail seen only in flight.

Female: similar to male, but with tan chin and lacking white tail band

Juvenile: same as adult

Nest: no nest; lays eggs on ground, usually on rocks, or on rooftop; 1 brood per year

Eggs: 2; cream with lavender markings

Incubation: 19-20 days; female and male incubate

Fledging: 20-21 days; female and male feed young

Migration: complete, to South America

Food: insects caught in air

Compare: Much larger than Chimney Swift (pg. 77). Look for the obvious white wing bars of Common Nighthawk.

Stan's Notes: Usually only seen flying at dusk or after sunset, but not uncommon during the day. Prolific insect eater. One of the first birds to migrate each autumn. More common in the city than country. Prefers gravel rooftops for nesting. Very noisy birds, repeating a "peenting" call during flight. Alternates slow wing beats with bursts of quick wing beats. Males' distinctive springtime mating ritual is a steep diving flight terminated with a loud popping noise.

Lesser Yellowlegs
Tringa flavipes

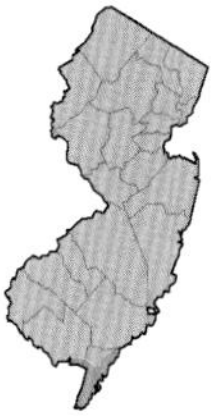

MIGRATION
WINTER

Size: 10-11" (25-28 cm)

Male: Typical sandpiper-type bird with brown back and wings, and lightly streaked white breast and belly. Thin, straight black bill and long yellow legs.

Female: same as male

Juvenile: same as adult

Nest: ground; female builds; 1 brood per year

Eggs: 3-4; yellowish with brown markings

Incubation: 22-23 days; male and female incubate

Fledging: 18-20 days; male and female lead young to food

Migration: complete, to South America

Food: aquatic insects

Compare: Nearly a carbon copy of Greater Yellowlegs (pg. 143), only smaller with shorter bill.

Stan's Notes: Usually seen in large flocks, they comb shorelines and mud flats looking for aquatic insects. They use their long straight bills to pluck insects and tiny fish from water. Very shy bird that quite often moves into the water prior to taking flight. Has a variety of "flight" notes that it gives when taking off. A member of the group of sandpipers called Tattlers, all of which scream alarm calls when taking flight. Most often seen in head down, tail up position, walking along, looking to snatch up something to eat. Nests on marshes in spruce forests of central Alaska and central Canada. Nest is a simple depression atop a mound of earth. Migrates later than Greater Yellowlegs in spring and earlier in fall.

Brown Thrasher
Toxostoma rufum

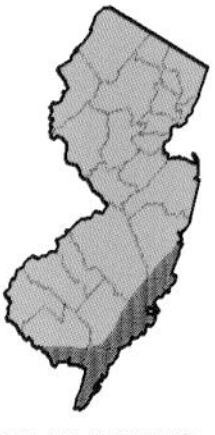

YEAR-ROUND
SUMMER

Size: 11" (28 cm)

Male: A rusty red bird with long tail and heavily streaked chest and belly. Two white wing bars. Long curved bill and bright yellow eye.

Female: same as male

Juvenile: same as adult, eye color grayish

Nest: cup; female and male build; 2 broods per year

Eggs: 4-5; pale blue with brown markings

Incubation: 11-14 days; female and male incubate

Fledging: 10-13 days; female and male feed young

Migration: complete, to southern states

Food: insects, fruit

Compare: Slightly larger in size and similar in shape to the American Robin (pg. 215) and Gray Catbird (pg. 211), but the Thrasher has a streaked chest and rusty color. Similar rusty color as Fox Sparrow (pg. 107), but Brown Thrasher is larger and thinner.

Stan's Notes: Prodigious songsters, they are often found in thick shrubs where they sing deliberate musical phrases, repeating each twice. The male has the largest documented song repertoire of all North American birds, with over 1,100 song types. Often seen quickly flying in and out of thick or dense shrubs.

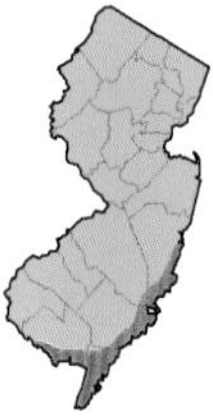

YEAR-ROUND
SUMMER

KILLDEER
Charadrius vociferus

Size: 11" (28 cm)

Male: An upland shorebird with two black bands around neck like a necklace. Brown back and white belly. Bright reddish orange rump, visible in flight.

Female: same as male

Juvenile: similar to adult, but only one neck band

Nest: ground; male builds; 2 broods per year

Eggs: 3-5; tan with brown markings

Incubation: 24-28 days; male and female incubate

Fledging: 25 days; male and female lead young to food

Migration: complete, to southern states, Mexico and Central America

Food: insects

Compare: Only shorebird with two black neck bands.

Stan's Notes: Known for its broken wing impression to draw intruders away from nest. Once clear of the nest, the bird takes flight. Young look like yellow cotton balls on stilts. Able to follow parents and peck for insects soon after birth. Nests are only a slight depression in a gravel area, often very difficult to see. Has a very distinctive "kill-jer" call. Often found in vacant fields or along railroads. Technically classified as a shorebird, but doesn't live at the shore.

male

female

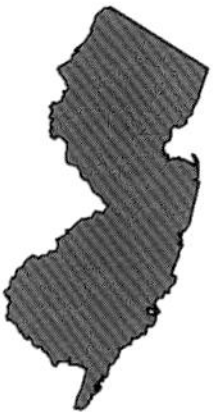

YEAR-ROUND

American Kestrel
Falco sparverius

Size: 10-12" (25-30 cm)

Male: Rusty brown back and tail. White chest with dark spots. Double black vertical lines on white face. Males have blue gray wings. Distinctive wide black band with white edge on tip of rusty tail.

Female: similar to male, slightly larger, but with rusty brown wings and dark bands on tail

Juvenile: same as adult

Nest: cavity; doesn't build nest within; 1 brood per year

Eggs: 4-5; white with brown markings

Incubation: 29-31 days; male and female incubate

Fledging: 30-31 days; female and male feed young

Migration: complete, to southern states and Central America, small percentage do not migrate

Food: insects, small mammals and birds, reptiles

Compare: Similar to other falcons. Look for the two vertical black stripes on face of Kestrel. No other small bird of prey has rusty-colored back or tail.

Stan's Notes: Formerly called Sparrow Hawk due to its small size. Seen hovering near roads before diving for prey. Adapts quickly to a wooden nest box. Has pointed swept-back wings seen in flight. Perches nearly upright. Kestrels are rare raptors in that the males and females have quite different markings. Watch for them to pump their tails up and down after landing on perches.

female
male

Northern Flicker

Colaptes auratus

YEAR-ROUND

Size: 12" (30 cm)

Male: Brown and black woodpecker with a large white rump patch visible only when flying. Black necklace above a speckled breast. Red spot on nape of neck and black mustache.

Female: same as male, lacking black mustache

Juvenile: same as adult

Nest: cavity; female and male excavate; 1 brood per year

Eggs: 5-8; white, unmarked

Incubation: 11-14 days; female and male incubate

Fledging: 25-28 days; female and male feed young

Migration: complete, to southern states

Food: insects, especially ants

Compare: The Red-bellied Woodpecker (pg. 35) has a black-and-white zebra-striped back, a red patch on head and lacks mustache. Flickers are the only brown-backed woodpeckers in New Jersey.

Stan's Notes: The flicker is the only woodpecker to regularly feed on the ground, preferring ants and beetles. Produces an antacid saliva to neutralize the acidic defense of ants. Males usually select nest site, which takes up to 12 days to excavate. Flashes golden yellow under wings and tail in flight. Undulates deeply in flight while giving a loud "wacka-wacka" call.

YEAR-ROUND

MOURNING DOVE
Zenaida macroura

Size: 12" (30 cm)

Male: Smooth fawn-colored dove with black spots on wings and tail. Single black spot behind and below eye. Pointed wedge-shaped tail with white edges. Gray patch on the head. Iridescent pink, green around neck.

Female: similar to male, lacks iridescent neck feathers

Juvenile: spotted and streaked, called a squab

Nest: platform; female and male build; 2 broods per year

Eggs: 2; white, unmarked

Incubation: 13-14 days; male and female incubate, male during day, female at night

Fledging: 12-14 days; female and male feed young

Migration: partial migrator, moves around to find food, or to southern states

Food: seeds, will come to seed feeders

Compare: Smaller than Rock Dove (pg. 223), lacking its wide range of color combinations.

Stan's Notes: Mourning Doves tend to mate for life, roughly seven to ten years. They build a flimsy platform nest of twigs that often falls apart in a storm. Ground feeders, look for heads bobbing as they walk. Parents feed the young a regurgitated liquid called crop-milk for the first few days of life. One of the few birds to drink without lifting head, same as Rock Dove. Name comes from its mournful cooing. Listen for characteristic whistling sound when they fly. This is caused by wind rushing through wing feathers.

male pg. 39
female

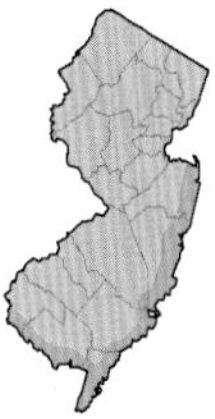

MIGRATION
WINTER

BUFFLEHEAD
Bucephala albeola

Size: 13-15" (33-38 cm)

Female: Brownish gray duck with dark brown head and white patch on cheek, just behind eye.

Male: striking black and white duck with a head that shines green purple in sunlight, large white bonnet-like patch on back of head

Juvenile: similar to female

Nest: cavity; female lines former woodpecker cavity; 1 brood per year

Eggs: 8-10; ivory to olive without markings

Incubation: 29-31 days; female incubates

Fledging: 50-55 days; female leads young to food

Migration: complete, to southern states and Central America

Food: aquatic insects

Compare: The female Bufflehead commonly confused with female Common Goldeneye (pg. 159), which lacks Bufflehead's white ear marking.

Stan's Notes: A common diving duck, Buffleheads travel amongst other ducks. Most commonly found in sheltered bays and coastal harbors, it is also found inland on rivers and lakes. Doesn't nest in New Jersey. Unlike other ducks, young remain in nests for up to two days before venturing out with their mothers. Female is very territorial and remains with the same mate for many years.

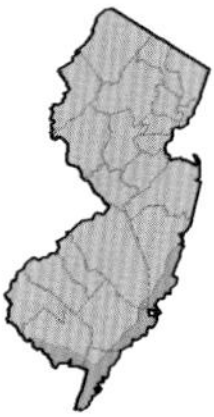

MIGRATION
WINTER

GREATER YELLOWLEGS
Tringa melanoleuca

Size: 14" (36 cm)

Male: A tall bird with bulbous head and long thin bill, slightly turned up. Gray streaking on chest and white belly. Long yellow legs.

Female: same as male

Juvenile: same as adult

Nest: ground; female builds; 1 brood per year

Eggs: 3-4; off-white with brown markings

Incubation: 22-23 days; female and male incubate

Fledging: 18-20 days; male and female feed young

Migration: complete, to southern states and South America

Food: small fish, aquatic insects

Compare: Nearly identical to the Lesser Yellowlegs (pg. 129), but larger, and with a longer and upturned bill.

Stan's Notes: A common shorebird identified by slightly upturned bill and long yellow legs, often seen resting on one leg. Its long legs carry it through deep water. Nests on the ground near water on the northern tundra of Labrador and Newfoundland. Often seen feeding by rushing forward through the water, plowing its bill or swinging it from side to side, catching small insects or fish. A skittish bird quick to give an alarm call, causing flocks to take flight. Quite often moves into the water prior to taking flight. Has a variety of "flight" notes that it gives when taking off.

female
male pg. 15

YEAR-ROUND

Boat-tailed Grackle
Quiscalus major

Size: 14" (36 cm), female
16" (40 cm), male

Female: Brown chest and head with nearly black wings and tail, lacking any iridescence.

Male: iridescent blue-black bird with a long tail and bright yellow eye

Juvenile: similar to adult

Nest: cup; female builds; 2 broods per year

Eggs: 2-4; pale greenish blue, brown markings

Incubation: 13-15 days; female incubates

Fledging: 12-15 days; female feeds young

Migration: non-migrator, moves around to find food

Food: insects, berries, seeds, fish

Compare: Female Boat-tailed Grackle fairly distinctive and not confused with many other birds. The male Boat-tailed is similar to the male Common Grackle (pg. 11), but the Boat-tailed has a distinctive long tail.

Stan's Notes: A bird of coastal saltwater marshes, it has only recently expanded its range into New Jersey in the last 40 years. A noisy bird that gives several harsh, high-pitched calls and several squeaks. Nests in small colonies. Boat-taileds on the Gulf coast have dark eyes, while the Atlantic coast birds have bright yellow eyes. Eats a wide variety of foods from grains to fish. Sometimes seen picking insects off backs of cattle. Will also visit bird feeders. Makes a cup nest with mud or cow dung.

male

female

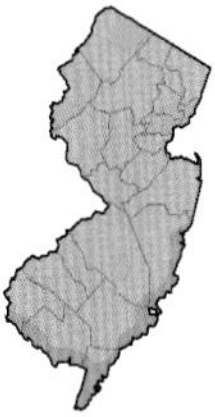

MIGRATION
SUMMER
WINTER

Green-winged Teal

Anas crecca

Size: 15" (38 cm)

Male: A chestnut head with a dark green patch behind the eye extending down to nape of the neck and outlined in white. Gray body with a butter yellow tail.

Female: light brown with black spots, small black bill

Juvenile: same as adult

Nest: ground; female builds; 1 brood per year

Eggs: 8-10; creamy white without markings

Incubation: 21-23 days; female incubates

Fledging: 32-34 days; female teaches young to feed

Migration: complete, to East coast and southern states

Food: aquatic plants and insects

Compare: Male Green-winged Teal is not as colorful as the male Wood Duck (pg. 157). Female Green-winged Teal is very similar to other female teals, but it has a smaller bill and green patch on wing (speculum).

Stan's Notes: One of the smallest dabbling ducks, tipping forward in the water to glean aquatic insects and plants from the bottom of shallow ponds. A common migrant and winter resident in New Jersey. Very few seen in summer. An early spring migrant, reaching New Jersey in March to April and again in autumn in October to November. Will feed in fields but returns to shallow ponds. Green speculum most obvious when in flight.

male pg. 41
female

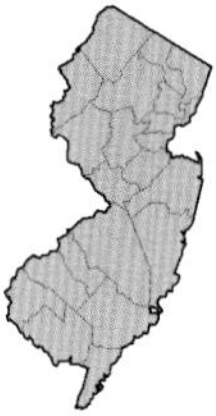

MIGRATION

LESSER SCAUP
Aythya affinis

Size: 16-17" (40-43 cm)

Female: An overall brown duck with a white patch at base of a light gray bill.

Male: white and gray, the chest and head appear nearly black; in direct sun, head appears purple with green highlights

Juvenile: same as female

Nest: ground; female builds; 1 brood per year

Eggs: 8-14; olive buff without markings

Incubation: 22-28 days; female incubates

Fledging: 45-50 days; female teaches young to feed

Migration: complete, to the southern states, northern South America, Central America

Food: aquatic plants and insects

Compare: The female Lesser Scaup nearly identical to the slightly larger, but less common, female Greater Scaup (pg. 155).

Stan's Notes: A common diving duck in New Jersey. Often seen in large flocks numbering in the thousands on area lakes, ponds and sewage lagoons. Usually only seen during migrations in late February and again in October. When observed in flight, note the bold white stripe under the wings. Has an interesting baby-sitting arrangement in which the young form groups tended by one to three adult females.

soaring

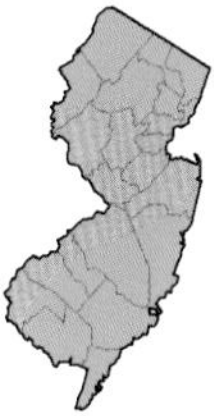

BROAD-WINGED HAWK
Buteo platypterus

Size: 14-19" (36-48 cm)

Male: A hawk slightly smaller than the American Crow, the Broad-winged has a brown back and rusty red barring on chest. Tail has two or three wide black-and-white bands. White under wings, with black "fingertips" when seen in flight.

Female: same as male

Juvenile: tail bands narrower and more numerous, brown-streaked chest and belly

Nest: platform; female and male build, but female finishes; 1 brood per year

Eggs: 2-3; off-white with brown markings

Incubation: 28-32 days; female incubates, male feeds female during incubation

Fledging: 34-35 days; female and male feed young

Migration: complete, to Central and South Americas

Food: small mammals, small birds, large insects, snakes, frogs

Compare: Similar in size to Cooper's Hawk (pg. 225), but with wider, shorter tail. Larger than Sharp-shinned Hawk (pg. 221). Note alternating white and black tail bands.

Stan's Notes: A very common hawk in New Jersey. Often seen in large groups (kettles) migrating early in autumn. Massive migration provides a spectacular sight. Spends most of its time hunting snakes, small birds and frogs in dense woodland. Short round wings propel it through dense woods.

female
male pg. 43

Hooded Merganser
Lophodytes cucullatus

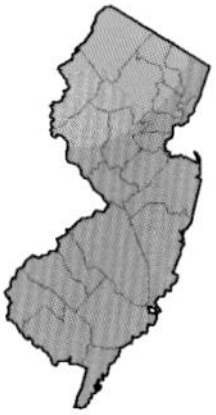

Size: 16-19" (40-48 cm)

Female: A sleek brown and rust bird with a red head and ragged "hair" on back of head. Gray body. Long, thin brown bill.

Male: same size and shape as female, but black back and rust sides, crest "hood" raises to reveal large white patch, long black bill

Juvenile: similar to female

Nest: cavity; female lines former woodpecker hole; 1 brood per year

Eggs: 10-12; white, unmarked

Incubation: 32-33 days; female incubates

Fledging: 71 days; female feeds young

Migration: complete, to Gulf coast and Mexico

Food: small fish, aquatic insects

Compare: Smaller than female Common Merganser (pg. 261) and lacking white chest.

Stan's Notes: Not as common as the Common Merganser, the male Hooded Merganser can voluntarily raise and lower the crest on its head to show off the large white patch. Females will "dump" eggs into other female Hooded Mergansers' nests, resulting in 20 to 25 eggs in some nests. Mergansers have been known to share a nesting cavity with Common Goldeneyes and Wood Ducks sitting side by side.

male pg. 45
female

GREATER SCAUP
Aythya marila

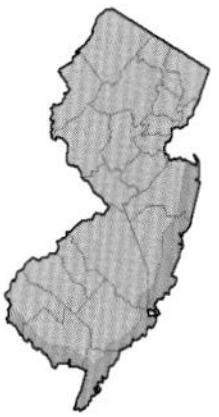

MIGRATION
WINTER

Size: 18" (45 cm)

Female: An overall brown duck with a darker head and a bold white patch at base of bill. Might show a white patch just behind eye. Top of head rounded.

Male: mostly black and white, black head shines green in direct light, has bright white sides and a gray back, light blue bill with a black tip, rounded head

Juvenile: similar to adult

Nest: ground; female builds; 1 brood per year

Eggs: 7-10; greenish-olive, unmarked

Incubation: 24-28 days; female incubates

Fledging: 45-50 days; female teaches young to feed

Migration: complete, along East and Gulf coasts

Food: aquatic plants and insects

Compare: Very similar to female Lesser Scaup (pg. 149). Has a rounded head vs. the Lesser's more pointed head. Female Greater Scaup has a bold white patch at base of bill.

Stan's Notes: Can be one of the most common ducks during winter in coastal New Jersey. They arrive in early October, leave by mid-April and don't nest in the state. With a ratio of about ten to one, Greater Scaups are by far more common than Lesser Scaups. Greater Scaups prefer saltwater, while the Lesser Scaups seem to prefer fresh water. Most abundant on large saltwater bays. Breeds in northern Canada and Alaska.

male pg. 235
female

Wood Duck
Aix sponsa

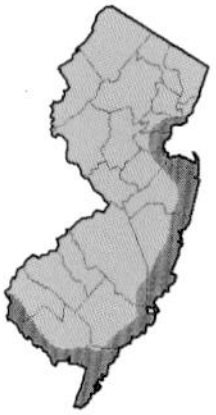

Size: 17-20" (43-50 cm)

Female: A small brown dabbling duck. Bright white eye ring and not so obvious crest. Blue patch on wing is often hidden.

Male: highly ornamented with a green head and crest, red eye, patterned with white and black, rusty chest and white belly

Juvenile: same as female

Nest: cavity; female lines former woodpecker cavity; 1 brood per year

Eggs: 10-15; creamy white, unmarked

Incubation: 28-36 days; female incubates

Fledging: 56-68 days; female teaches young to feed

Migration: complete, to southern states

Food: aquatic insects, plants, seeds

Compare: Smaller than the female Northern Shoveler (pg. 161) and lacks the long wide bill. Smaller than the female Mallard (pg. 173), which lacks Wood Duck's white eye ring.

Stan's Notes: A common duck of quiet, shallow backwater ponds. Nests in old woodpecker holes or nest boxes. Often seen flying deep within a forest or perched high up on branches of trees. Female takes flight with loud squealing call and enters nest cavity from full flight. Will lay eggs in neighboring female nest, called egg dumping, resulting in some clutches in excess of 20 eggs. Young remain in nest cavity only 24 hours after hatching, then jump from up to 30 feet to the ground or water to follow their mother. After that, they never return to the nest.

female
male pg. 51

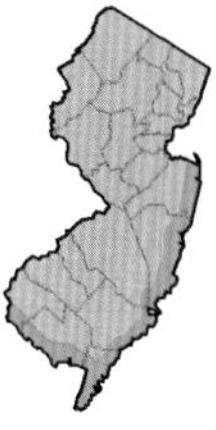

MIGRATION
WINTER

Common Goldeneye
Bucephala clangula

Size: 18½-20" (47-50 cm)

Female: A brown and gray duck with a large dark brown head, gray body, a white collar and bright golden eyes.

Male: mostly white duck with black back, a large, puffy green head, with a large white spot in front of each bright golden eye

Juvenile: same as female

Nest: cavity; female lines former woodpecker cavity; 1 brood per year

Eggs: 8-10; light green without markings

Incubation: 28-32 days; female incubates

Fledging: 56-59 days; female leads young to food

Migration: complete, to southern states

Food: aquatic plants, insects

Compare: Similar to, but larger than, the brown and white female Lesser Scaup (pg. 149). Look for female Goldeneye's dark brown head and white collar.

Stan's Notes: Known for their loud whistling, which is produced by their wings in flight. In late winter and early spring, males often attract females through elaborate displays, throwing their heads backwards while uttering a single raspy note. Females will lay eggs in other goldeneye nests, resulting in some mothers incubating up to 30 eggs. Received its common name from its obvious bright golden eyes.

male pg. 239
female

Northern Shoveler
Anas clypeata

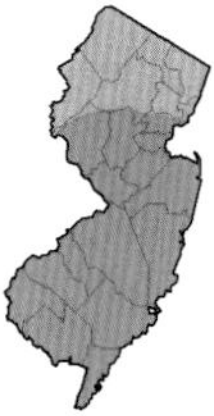

Size: 20" (50 cm)

Female: A medium-sized brown duck speckled with black. Blue wing patch. Has an extraordinarily large spoon-shaped bill, almost always held pointed towards the water.

Male: same spoon-shaped bill, iridescent green head, rusty sides and a white breast

Juvenile: same as female

Nest: ground; female builds; 1 brood per year

Eggs: 9-12; olive, unmarked

Incubation: 22-25 days; female incubates

Fledging: 30-60 days; female leads young to food

Migration: complete, to southern states and Central America

Food: aquatic insects, plants

Compare: Similar to female Mallard (pg. 173). Check for spoon-shaped bill. Larger than the average female Wood Duck (pg. 157), lacking white eye ring.

Stan's Notes: Seen in small flocks of five to ten, swimming low in water with large bills always pointed towards water, as if they're too heavy to lift. More commonly seen during spring migration. Feeds primarily by filtering tiny plants and insects from the water's surface with bill.

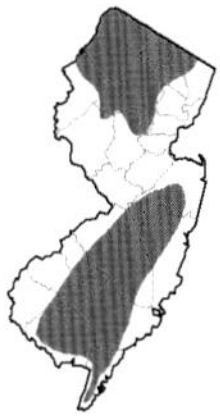
YEAR-ROUND

Barred Owl
Strix varia

Size: 20-24" (50-60 cm)

Male: A chunky brown and gray owl with dark horizontal barring on chest, and vertical streaking on belly. Large head with dark brown eyes.

Female: same as male, only slightly larger

Juvenile: same as adult

Nest: cavity; no nesting material brought in; 1 brood per year

Eggs: 2-3; white, unmarked

Incubation: 28-33 days; female incubates

Fledging: 42-44 days; female and male feed young

Migration: non-migrator

Food: mammals, small birds

Compare: Lacks the "horns" of the Great Horned Owl (pg. 167). It's our only owl with dark eyes. About twice the size of the tiny Eastern Screech-Owl (pg. 213).

Stan's Notes: A very common owl that can often be seen hunting during the day. Prefers dense woodland with sparse undergrowth. Can be attracted with a simple nest box with a large opening attached to a tree. The young will stay with the parents for up to four months after fledging. Often sounds like a dog barking just before giving an eight-hoot call that sounds like, "Who-cooks-for-you? Who-cooks-for-you?" Great Horned Owl sounds like, "Hoo-hoo-hoo-hoooo!"

soaring

YEAR-ROUND

Red-tailed Hawk
Buteo jamaicensis

Size: 19-25" (48-63 cm); up to 4-foot wingspan

Male: A large hawk with an amazing variety of colors from bird to bird, from chocolate brown to nearly all white. Often brown with white breast and distinctive brown belly band. Rust red tail usually only seen from above. Underside of wing white with small dark patch on leading edge near shoulder.

Female: same as male, often larger

Juvenile: similar to adult, lacking red tail, speckled chest

Nest: platform; male and female build; 1 brood per year

Eggs: 2-3; white, unmarked or occasionally marked with brown

Incubation: 30-35 days; female and male incubate

Fledging: 45-46 days; male and female feed young

Migration: partial migrator, to southern states, small percentage do not migrate

Food: mice, birds, snakes, insects

Compare: Nearly twice the size of the Sharp-shinned Hawk (pg. 221).

Stan's Notes: The most common hawk of open country and cities, often seen perched on freeway light posts. Look for it circling above open fields searching for prey. Will return to the same nest site each year. Doesn't develop red tail until second year.

Great Horned Owl
Bubo virginianus

YEAR-ROUND

Size: 20-25" (50-63 cm)

Male: A robust brown "horned" owl with bright yellow eyes and V-shaped white bib.

Female: same as male, only slightly larger

Juvenile: similar to adult

Nest: no nest; takes over the nests of crows, Great Blue Herons and hawks, or uses partial cavities; 1 brood per year

Eggs: 2; white, unmarked

Incubation: 26-30 days; female incubates

Fledging: 30-35 days; male and female feed young

Migration: non-migrator

Food: small mammals, birds, snakes, insects

Compare: The Barred Owl (pg. 163) has no "horns" and dark eyes. Over twice the size of the Eastern Screech-Owl (pg. 213).

Stan's Notes: Earliest nesting bird in New Jersey, it lays eggs in January and February. Has excellent hearing; able to hear a mouse moving under a foot of snow. "Ears" are actually tufts of feathers (horns) and have nothing to do with hearing. Not able to turn head all the way around. Wing feathers are ragged on the end, resulting in a silent flight. Eyelids close from the top down, like humans. Fearless, it is one of the few animals that will kill skunks and porcupines. Because of this, it is sometimes called Flying Tiger.

male

female

YEAR-ROUND

AMERICAN BLACK DUCK
Anas rubripes

Size: 23" (58 cm)

Male: Overall dark brown, sometimes appearing nearly black. Neck and head are lighter in color. Yellow bill and orange legs. White wing linings contrast sharply with dark wings when in flight. Violet patch (speculum) on wing is bordered in black.

Female: same as male, except bill is dull green with black flecks

Juvenile: same as adult

Nest: ground; female builds; 1 brood per year

Eggs: 8-10; creamy white to greenish buff

Incubation: 26-29 days; female incubates

Fledging: 16-17 days; female teaches young to feed

Migration: complete, to southern states

Food: aquatic plants, seeds

Compare: Both the male and female American Black Ducks are very similar to the female Mallard (pg. 173), but the female Mallard has an orange bill unlike the dull green bill of the female American Black Duck. Mallard has a blue patch (speculum) bordered by white.

Stan's Notes: Hybridizes (mates) with Mallards, producing a bird lacking the Mallard's brilliant colors. Formerly the most abundant duck breeding in New Jersey and the U.S., the Mallard is now more common. Female builds nest in grass tall enough to conceal herself. Male leaves female while she is still incubating the eggs. Young are able to leave the nest one to three hours after hatching.

male pg. 227

female

NORTHERN HARRIER

Circus cyaneus

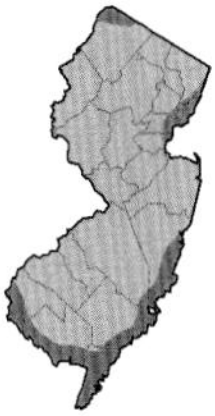

Size: 24" (60 cm)

Female: A slim, low-flying hawk. Dark brown back with brown-streaked breast and belly. Large white rump patch. Narrow black bands across tail. Tips of wings black.

Male: silver gray with large white rump patch and white belly, faint narrow bands across tail, tips of wings black

Juvenile: similar to female, with orange breast

Nest: platform; female and male build; 1 brood per year

Eggs: 4-8; bluish white, unmarked

Incubation: 31-32 days; female incubates

Fledging: 30-35 days; male and female feed young

Migration: complete, southern states, Central America

Food: mice, snakes

Compare: Slimmer than Red-tailed Hawk (pg. 165). Look for black bands on tail and a white rump patch.

Stan's Notes: One of the easiest hawks to identify. Harriers glide just above ground, following the contours of the land while searching for prey. Wings are held just above the horizontal position, tilting back and forth in the wind, similar to Turkey Vultures. Formerly called Marsh Hawk due to its habit of hunting over marshes. Nests on the ground. At all ages, the Northern Harrier has distinctive owl-like face disks.

male pg. 243
female

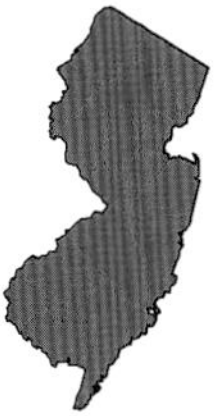

YEAR-ROUND

MALLARD

Anas platyrhynchos

Size: 27-28" (69-71 cm)

Female: All-brown duck with orange and black bill, and small blue and white wing mark, called a speculum.

Male: large, bulbous green head, white necklace, rust brown or chestnut chest, combination of gray and white on sides, yellow bill, legs and feet

Juvenile: same as female, but with yellow bill

Nest: ground; female builds; 1 brood per year

Eggs: 7-10; greenish to whitish, unmarked

Incubation: 26-30 days; female incubates

Fledging: 42-52 days; female leads young to food

Migration: complete, to southern states, small percentage non-migrator

Food: seeds, plants, aquatic insects, ground feeders offering corn

Compare: The female Northern Shoveler (pg. 161) is smaller and has a large spoon-shaped bill. Female Wood Duck (pg. 157) is smaller and has white eye ring.

Stan's Notes: Familiar duck of lakes and ponds. Will return to place of birth. The name "Mallard" comes from the Latin *masculus*, meaning "male," referring to the habit of males not taking part in raising ducklings. Both male and female have white tails and white underwings. Black central tail feathers of male curl upward.

male

female

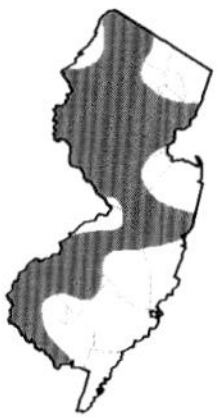

Ring-necked Pheasant
Phasianus colchicus

Size: 30-36" (76-90 cm), male, including tail
21-25" (53-63 cm), female, including tail

Male: Golden brown body with long tail. White ring around neck with purple, green, blue and red head.

Female: smaller, less flamboyant all-brown bird with long tail

Juvenile: similar to female, with shorter tail

Nest: ground; female builds; 1 brood per year

Eggs: 8-10; olive brown, unmarked

Incubation: 23-25 days; female incubates

Fledging: 11-12 days; female leads young to food

Migration: non-migrator

Food: insects, seeds, fruit, will come to ground feeders

Compare: The Ring-necked Pheasant has a long tail, and male is brightly colored.

Stan's Notes: Introduced from China in the late 1800s. Now common throughout the U.S. Like many game birds, their numbers vary greatly, making them common some years and scarce others. The name "Ring-necked" refers to the thin white ring around the male's neck. The name "Pheasant" comes from the Greek word *phaisianos*, meaning "a bird of the River Phasis," which is now known as the River Rioni, located in Europe. Listen for the male's cackling call to attract females.

Wild Turkey
Meleagris gallopavo

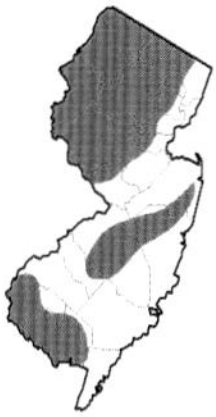

YEAR-ROUND

Size: 36-48" (90-120 cm)

Male: Large, plump brown and bronze bird with striking blue and red bare head. Fan tail and long, straight black beard in center of chest. Spurs on legs.

Female: thinner and less striking than male, usually lacking breast beard

Juvenile: same as adult

Nest: ground; female builds; 1 brood per year

Eggs: 10-12; buff white with dull brown markings

Incubation: 27-28 days; female incubates

Fledging: 6-10 days; female leads young to food

Migration: non-migrator

Food: insects, seeds, fruit

Compare: This bird is distinctive and unlikely to be confused with others.

Stan's Notes: Eliminated from New Jersey by 1844 due to market hunting and loss of habitat, they were reintroduced in the 1960-80s. Males hold "harems" of up to 20 females. Strong fliers, they can approach 60 mph. Able to fly straight up, then away. Eyesight three times better than humans. Their hearing is also excellent; able to hear competing males up to one mile away. Nearly became our national bird, but lost by one vote to the Bald Eagle. They roost in trees at night. The bird from which the domestic turkey was bred. Largest game bird in New Jersey. Males are called toms, females are hens and the young are called poults.

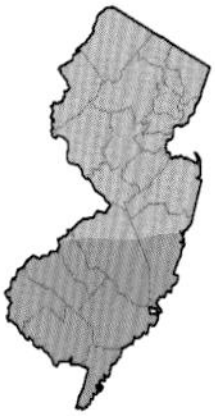

MIGRATION
WINTER

Ruby-crowned Kinglet
Regulus calendula

Size: 4" (10 cm)

Male: Small, teardrop-shaped gray green bird with two white wing bars and a hidden ruby-colored crown. White eye ring.

Female: same as male, lacks ruby crown

Juvenile: same as adult

Nest: pendulous; female builds; 1 brood per year

Eggs: 4-5; white with brown markings

Incubation: 11-12 days; female incubates

Fledging: 11-12 days; female and male feed young

Migration: complete, to southern states, Mexico and Central America

Food: insects, berries

Compare: Similar to the Golden-crowned Kinglet (pg. 181), but crown is ruby colored.

Stan's Notes: Most commonly seen during spring and autumn migrations. It takes a quick eye to see the male's ruby crown. Look for small bird flitting around thick shrubs low to the ground. The name "Kinglet" comes from the Anglo-Saxon word *cyning*, or "king," referring to its ruby crown, and the diminutive suffix "let," meaning "small." The second smallest bird in New Jersey. Builds an unusual pendulous (sac-like) nest, intricately woven and suspended from a branch overlapped by leaves. Usually the nest is hung high in mature trees. It is decorated on the outside with colored lichens and mosses stuck together with spider webs.

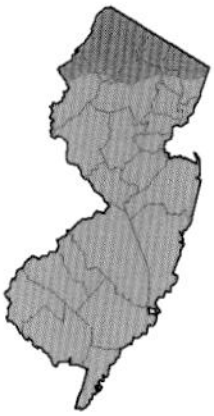

YEAR-ROUND
WINTER

Golden-crowned Kinglet
Regulus satrapa

Size: 4" (10 cm)

Male: A tiny, plump gray green bird with a distinctive yellow and orange patch with black border on crown. White eyebrow mark. Two white wing bars.

Female: same as male, but has a yellow crown, lacking any orange

Juvenile: same as adult

Nest: pendulous; female builds; 1-2 broods a year

Eggs: 5-9; white or creamy with brown markings

Incubation: 14-15 days; female incubates

Fledging: 14-19 days; female and male feed young

Migration: complete, to southern states, Mexico and Central America

Food: insects, fruit, tree sap

Compare: Similar to Ruby-crowned Kinglet (pg. 179), but Golden-crowned has an obvious crown. Smaller than the female American Goldfinch (pg. 283), which lacks any crown marking.

Stan's Notes: Often seen in flocks that include chickadees, nuthatches, woodpeckers and Ruby-crowned Kinglets. Has a habit of flicking its wings when moving around. Unusual hanging nest is often made of moss, lichens and spider webs, and lined with bark and feathers. Can have so many eggs in its small nest that eggs are in two layers. Drinks tree sap and feeds by gleaning insects from trees. Can be very tame and approachable.

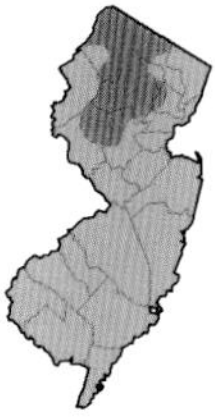

Red-breasted Nuthatch
Sitta canadensis

Size: 4½" (11 cm)

Male: Small gray-backed bird with a black cap and prominent eye line. Rust red breast and belly.

Female: gray cap, pale undersides

Juvenile: same as female

Nest: cavity; female builds; 1 brood per year

Eggs: 5-6; white with red brown markings

Incubation: 11-12 days; female incubates

Fledging: 14-20 days; female and male feed young

Migration: irruptive, moves around the state to find food

Food: insects, seeds, will come to seed and suet feeders

Compare: Smaller than the White-breasted Nuthatch (pg. 193), has a red breast instead of white.

Stan's Notes: Common during some winters and scarce during others, Red-breasted Nuthatch behaves like the White-breasted Nuthatch, climbing down tree trunks head-first. Similar to chickadees, visits seed feeders, quickly grabbing one seed and flying off to crack it open. Will wedge a seed into a crevice and pound it open with several sharp blows. The name "Nuthatch" comes from the Middle English moniker *nuthak*, referring to the bird's habit of wedging a seed into a crevice and hacking it open. Look for them in mature conifers, frequently extracting seeds from cones. Doesn't excavate cavity as a chickadee might; rather, it takes over a former woodpecker or chickadee cavity.

BLACK-CAPPED CHICKADEE
Poecile atricapilla

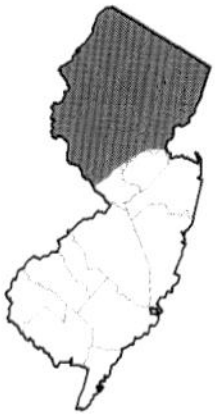

YEAR-ROUND

Size: 5" (13 cm)

Male: Familiar gray bird with a black cap and throat patch. White chest and a tan belly. Small white wing marks.

Female: same as male

Juvenile: same as adult

Nest: cavity; female and male build or excavate; 1 brood per year

Eggs: 5-7; white, fine brown markings

Incubation: 11-13 days; female and male incubate

Fledging: 14-18 days; female and male feed young

Migration: non-migrator

Food: insects, seeds, fruit, attracted to seed and suet feeders

Compare: Identical to Carolina Chickadee (pg. 187), except in song. Carolina's song is a higher and faster version of the Black-capped Chickadee's. Tufted Titmouse (pg. 197) is larger than Black-capped Chickadee and has a crest.

Stan's Notes: A common backyard bird that can be attracted with a simple nest box. Makes nest mostly of green moss and lined with animal fur. Usually the first bird to find a new bird feeder. Can have different calls in various regions. Can be easily tamed and hand fed. Needs to feed every day during winter; consequently seen foraging for food during even the worst winter storms.

Carolina Chickadee
Poecile carolinensis

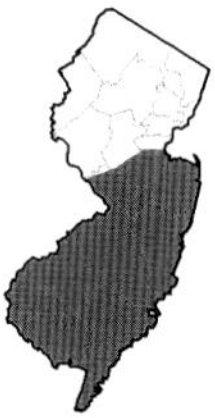

YEAR-ROUND

Size: 5" (13 cm)

Male: A mostly gray bird with a black cap and chin. White face and chest with a tan belly. Darker gray tail.

Female: same as male

Juvenile: same as adult

Nest: cavity; female and male build or excavate; 1-2 broods per year

Eggs: 5-7; white with reddish brown markings

Incubation: 11-12 days; female and male incubate

Fledging: 13-17 days; female and male feed young

Migration: non-migrator

Food: insects, seeds, fruit, comes to seed and suet feeders

Compare: Identical to the Black-capped Chickadee (pg. 185), except in song. Tufted Titmouse (pg. 197) has an erect crest, and lacks the black cap and chin.

Stan's Notes: A common bird of southern New Jersey. It will breed (hybridize) with the more northern Black-capped Chickadee where they meet. Can be attracted with a nest box with a 1¼-inch entrance hole. Females will give a loud snake-like hiss when disturbed on the nest. Often seen with other birds (mixed flock) during winter. A friendly bird that can be tamed and hand fed. Difficult to tell apart from the Black-capped Chickadee; best distinction is the song. Carolina's song is higher, faster version of the familiar "chika-dee-dee-dee-dee."

male

female

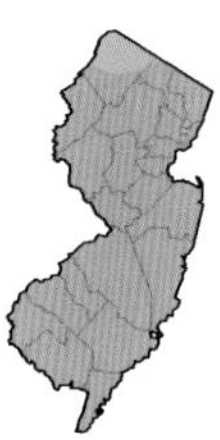

YELLOW-RUMPED WARBLER
Dendroica coronata

Size: 5-6" (13-15 cm)

Male: Slate gray bird with black mask and chest. Has yellow patch on head, flank and rump. White chin and belly. Two white wing bars.

Female: similar to male, duller in color, mostly brown and white with matching yellow patches

Juvenile: similar to female

Nest: cup; female builds; 2 broods per year

Eggs: 4-5; white with brown markings

Incubation: 12-13 days; female incubates

Fledging: 10-12 days; female and male feed young

Migration: complete, to southern states, Mexico and Central America

Food: insects, berries, rarely comes to suet feeders

Compare: Similar to other warblers, look for combination of yellow patches on head, flank and rump. Magnolia Warbler (pg. 287) is more yellow than Yellow-rumped Warbler. Prairie Warbler (pg. 291) has olive back with chestnut-colored streaks. Common Yellowthroat (pg. 285) has yellow breast, compared with Yellow-rumped Warbler's spots of yellow.

Stan's Notes: One of the only warblers to spend the winter in New Jersey, and one of the most common warblers, seen in flocks of hundreds during spring and fall migrations. Formerly called the Myrtle Warbler. Sometimes called Butter-butts due to yellow patch on rump. Males molt to a dull color similar to females each winter, retaining yellow patches. Familiar call is a robust "chip."

female pg. 93
male

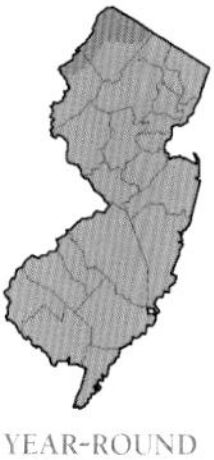

Dark-eyed Junco
Junco hyemalis

Size: 5½" (14 cm)

Male: A round bird with a slate gray-to-charcoal chest, head and back. White belly, pink bill and dark eye. Since outermost tail feathers are white, tail appears as a white V in flight.

Female: same as male, only tan-to-brown color

Juvenile: similar to female, with streaked chest and head

Nest: cup; female and male build; 2 broods per year

Eggs: 3-5; white with reddish brown markings

Incubation: 12-13 days; female incubates

Fledging: 10-13 days; male and female feed young

Migration: complete, all across United States

Food: seeds, insects, will come to seed feeders

Compare: Rarely confused with other birds. Large flocks come to feed under bird feeders.

Stan's Notes: One of New Jersey's most common winter birds. Usually seen on the ground in small flocks. Migrates from Canada to New Jersey and beyond. Small population stays year-round in northern New Jersey. Males tend to migrate farther south than females. Look for white outer tail feathers that flash in flight. Several species of juncos have now been combined into one, simply called Dark-eyed Junco. Most comfortable on the ground, juncos "double-scratch" with both feet to expose seeds and insects. Consume many weed seeds. A flocking bird, it adheres to a rigid social hierarchy with dominant birds chasing less dominant birds.

White-breasted Nuthatch
Sitta carolinensis

YEAR-ROUND

Size: 5-6" (13-15 cm)

Male: Slate gray bird with white belly, and black cap and neck. Long thin bill is slightly upturned. Chestnut-colored undertail.

Female: similar to male, gray cap and neck

Juvenile: same as adult

Nest: cavity; female and male build; 1 brood per year

Eggs: 5-7; white with brown markings

Incubation: 11-12 days; female incubates

Fledging: 13-14 days; female and male feed young

Migration: non-migrator

Food: insects, seeds, will come to seed and suet feeders

Compare: The Red-breasted Nuthatch (pg. 183) is smaller, and has rusty belly and distinctive black eye line.

Stan's Notes: The Nuthatch's habit of hopping head-first down tree trunks helps them see insects and eggs that birds climbing up the trunk might miss. The name "Nuthatch" comes from the Middle English moniker *nuthak*, referring to the bird's habit of wedging a seed into a crevice and hacking it open. Often seen in mixed flocks of chickadees and Downy Woodpeckers. Mated pairs remain together all year, defending their small territories. Listen for characteristic springtime call, "whi-whi-whi-whi," given during February and March. One of 17 worldwide nuthatch species. Incredible climbing agility comes from an extra long hind toe claw or nail, nearly twice the size of front toe claws.

breeding
winter

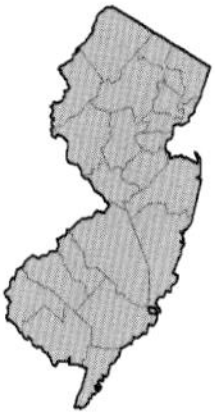

SEMIPALMATED SANDPIPER
Calidris pusilla

Size: 6" (15 cm)

Male: A plump gray shorebird with black legs and a short, straight, blunt-tipped black bill. Winter plumage of grayish brown head, neck and back, and white chest and eyebrow. Breeding plumage (usually seen in the Arctic) of brown head with some black and brown spots on the back, and a white belly.

Female: same as male

Juvenile: overall gray-brown with black spots

Nest: ground; male and female build; 1 brood per year

Eggs: 2-4; light yellow with brown markings

Incubation: 18-22 days; male and female incubate

Fledging: 18-20 days; male and female feed young

Migration: complete, to Bahamas and northern South America

Food: aquatic insects

Compare: Much smaller and darker gray than winter Sanderling (pg. 205).

Stan's Notes: The most common shorebird in New Jersey. Can be seen during spring migration (May to June), feeding on horseshoe crab eggs. Fall migration from July to August. Males do most of the care of young after hatching, since females abandon their families about two to three days after eggs hatch. Will retain same mate for several years. Nests in northern Canada and Alaska.

YEAR-ROUND

Tufted Titmouse
Baeolophus bicolor

Size: 6" (15 cm)

Male: Slate gray bird with a white chest and belly. Flanks washed in rusty brown. Gray legs and dark eyes. Pointed crest.

Female: same as male

Juvenile: same as adult

Nest: cavity, takes over former woodpecker hole; female builds; 2 broods per year

Eggs: 5-7; white with brown markings

Incubation: 13-14 days; female incubates

Fledging: 15-18 days; female and male feed young

Migration: non-migrator

Food: insects, seeds, fruit, comes to seed and suet feeders

Compare: Closely related to, but slightly larger than, the Black-capped Chickadee (pg. 185) and Carolina Chickadee (pg. 187). Chickadees lack crest of the Tufted Titmouse. Similar in size and color to the White-breasted Nuthatch (pg. 193), but Nuthatch doesn't have a crest.

Stan's Notes: Prefix "Tit" comes from a Scandinavian word meaning "little." Suffix "mouse" is derived from the Old English word *mase*, which means "bird." Simply translated, it is "a small bird." Notorious for pulling hair from sleeping dogs, cats and squirrels to line their nests. Attracted with nest boxes. Usually seen only one or two at a time. Male feeds female during courtship and nesting.

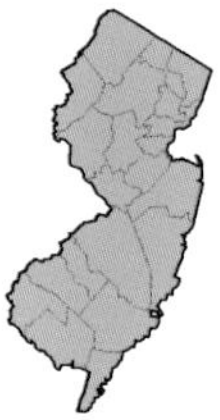

SUMMER

Eastern Phoebe
Sayornis phoebe

Size: 7" (18 cm)

Male: Gray green bird with dark wings, light olive green belly and a thin dark bill.

Female: same as male

Juvenile: same as adult

Nest: cup; female builds; 2 broods per year

Eggs: 4-5; white, unmarked

Incubation: 15-16 days; female incubates

Fledging: 15-16 days; male and female feed young

Migration: complete, to southern states and Mexico

Food: insects

Compare: Like most olive green birds, it is hard to distinguish any identifying markings. Eastern Phoebe lacks any white eye ring. Easier to identify by well-enunciated song, "fee-bee," or characteristic of hawking for insects.

Stan's Notes: A sparrow-sized bird often seen on the end of a dead branch. It sits waiting for a passing insect, flies out to catch it and then returns to the same branch, a process called hawking. Will build nest under the eaves of a house, under a bridge or in culverts. The nest, made of mud, grass and moss, is lined with hair and feathers. Name derived from its characteristic song, "fee-bee," repeated over and over from the tops of dead branches. Phoebe has a habit of pumping and spreading its tail when perched.

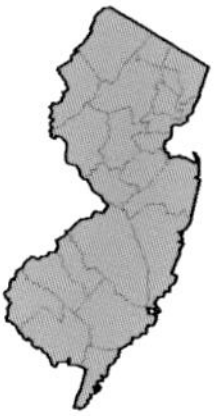

Eastern Kingbird
Tyrannus tyrannus

Size: 8" (20 cm)

Male: Mostly black gray bird with white belly and chin. Black head and tail with a distinctive white band across the end of the tail. Has a concealed red crown that is rarely seen.

Female: same as male

Juvenile: same as adult

Nest: cup; male and female build; 1 brood per year

Eggs: 3-4; white with brown markings

Incubation: 16-18 days; female incubates

Fledging: 16-18 days; female and male feed young

Migration: complete, to Central and South Americas

Food: insects, fruit

Compare: Rarely confused with other birds. Medium-sized bird, smaller than American Robin (pg. 215). Look for the white band along the end of the tail to identify.

Stan's Notes: A common bird of open fields and prairies. Perceived as having an attitude, acting unafraid of other birds and chasing the larger ones. Bold behavior gave rise to its common name, King. Perches on tall branches watching for insects. After flying out to catch them, returns to the same perch, a technique called hawking. Males and females return to mating grounds and will defend a territory together.

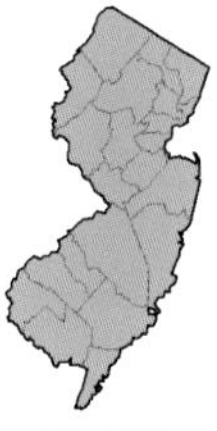
SUMMER

Great Crested Flycatcher
Myiarchus crinitus

Size: 8" (20 cm)

Male: Gray head with a prominent crest. Gray back and throat with a bright yellow belly extending down under reddish brown tail. Lower bill is yellow at base.

Female: same as male

Juvenile: same as adult

Nest: cavity; female and male build; 1 brood per year

Eggs: 4-6; white or buff with brown markings

Incubation: 13-15 days; female incubates

Fledging: 14-21 days; female and male feed young

Migration: complete, to Mexico and Central America

Food: insects, fruit

Compare: The Eastern Kingbird (pg. 201) has a white band across the tail. Similar to the Eastern Phoebe (pg. 199), but Great Crested Flycatcher has obvious crest and yellow belly.

Stan's Notes: A common bird of just about any wooded area, it lives high up in the trees, rarely coming to the ground. Often heard before seen. Feeds by gleaning insects from the leaves of trees. Nests in old woodpecker holes, but can be attracted to a nest box placed high in a tree with an entrance hole of 1½-2½ inches. Often stuffs nest with a collection of fur, feathers, string and snakeskins. Breeds throughout New Jersey. Flycatcher with the largest crest in the eastern U.S.

breeding
pg. 119
winter

SANDERLING
Calidris alba

Size: 8" (20 cm)

Male: Black legs and bill. Winter plumage of gray head and back, white belly and a white wing stripe shown only in flight. During winter, it's the lightest-colored sandpiper on the beach. During the breeding season (April to August), head, chest and back are rusty with a white belly.

Female: same as male

Juvenile: spotty black on head and back, with white belly, black legs and bill

Nest: ground; 1-2 broods per year

Eggs: 3-4; greenish-olive with brown markings

Incubation: 24-30 days; male and female incubate

Fledging: 16-17 days; female and male feed young

Migration: partial to complete, to East and Gulf coasts, South America and West Indies

Food: insects

Compare: Same size as the winter plumage Spotted Sandpiper (pg. 117).

Stan's Notes: One of the most common shorebirds in New Jersey. Can be seen in groups on sandy beaches, running out with each retreating wave to feed. Occasionally the female mates with several males (polyandry), resulting in males and the female incubating separate nests. Both sexes perform a distraction display if threatened. Nests in the Arctic tundra. Look for a flash of white on the wings when in flight. Declining in populations. Surveys show a more than 80 percent decline in numbers since the 1970s.

winter
breeding
pg. 121

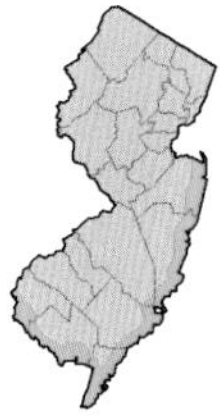

WINTER

Dunlin
Calidris alpina

Size: 8-9" (20-22.5 cm)

Male: Black legs. Stout bill curved slightly downward at the tip. Winter plumage of grayish brown back with light gray chest and white belly. Distinctive breeding plumage of rusty red back with a finely streaked chest and an obvious black patch on belly.

Female: slightly larger than male, with longer bill

Juvenile: slightly rusty back with spotty chest

Nest: ground; male and female build; 1 brood per year

Eggs: 2-4; olive-buff or blue-green with red-brown markings

Incubation: 21-22 days; male and female incubate, male during day, female at night

Fledging: 19-21 days; male feeds young, female often leaves before young fledge

Migration: complete, to the southern coastal states and East, Gulf and Central America coasts

Food: insects

Compare: Similar size as winter Sanderling (pg. 205), but Dunlin has a longer bill and is an overall darker gray.

Stan's Notes: Flights include heights of 100 feet with brief gliding alternating with shallow flutters, and rhythmic, repeating song. Males tend to fly farther south than females in winter. Huge flocks fly synchronously, twisting and turning, flashing their light and dark undersides.

male pg. 259
female

WINTER

Pine Grosbeak
Pinicola enucleator

Size: 9" (22.5 cm)

Female: A plump gray winter finch with a long dark tail. Dark wings with two white wing bars. Head and rump tinged dull yellow. Short, stubby, dark pointed bill.

Male: overall rosy red and gray

Juvenile: female juvenile similar to adult, but male juvenile has bit of red on head and rump

Nest: cup; female builds; 1 brood per year

Eggs: 4-5, bluish green, unmarked

Incubation: 13-15 days, female incubates

Fledging: 13-20 days, female and male feed young

Migration: non-migrator to irruptive, moves around to find food

Food: seeds, fruit, insects, will come to feeders

Compare: Much larger than the female Purple Finch (pg. 97) and female House Finch (pg. 83).

Stan's Notes: A winter finch throughout northern New Jersey in some years, and not so common in others. Often seen along roads or on the ground eating tiny grains of sand and dirt to aid in digestion. A seed eater that favors conifer woods, but also moves into deciduous woods where it relishes ash tree seeds. Flies with typical finch-like undulating pattern while calling a soft whistle. During breeding season both male and female develop a pouch in bottom of mouth to transport seeds to young. Very tame and approachable bird. Often seen bathing in fluffy snow.

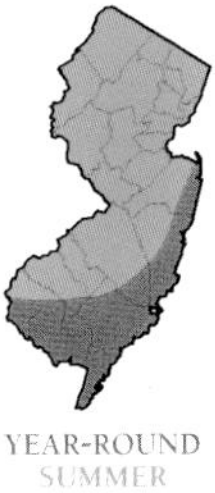

GRAY CATBIRD
Dumetella carolinensis

Size: 9" (22.5 cm)

Male: A handsome slate gray bird with a black crown. Long, thin black bill. Often seen with tail lifted, exposing chestnut-colored patch under tail.

Female: same as male

Juvenile: same as adult

Nest: cup; female and male build; 2 broods per year

Eggs: 4-6; blue green, unmarked

Incubation: 12-13 days; female incubates

Fledging: 10-11 days; female and male feed young

Migration: complete, to southern states

Food: insects, fruit

Compare: Larger than Eastern Phoebe (pg. 199), it lacks the Phoebe's olive belly. Similar size to Eastern Kingbird (pg. 201), but it lacks the Kingbird's white belly and white tail band.

Stan's Notes: A secretive bird that the Chippewa Indians named Bird That Cries With Grief due to its raspy call. Its call sounds like a house cat's mewing, hence its common name. Often mimics other birds, rarely repeating the same phrases. Will only nest in thick shrubs and is more often heard than seen. Quickly flies back into the shrubs when approached. If a cowbird introduces an egg into a catbird nest, the catbird will quickly break it, then eject it.

EASTERN SCREECH-OWL
Otus asio

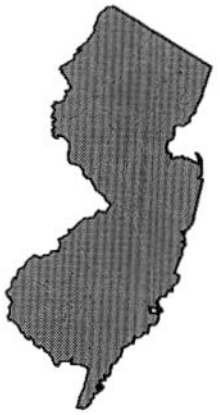

YEAR-ROUND

Size: 9" (22.5 cm)

Male: A small "eared" owl that occurs in one of two permanent color phases. Birds are either mottled with gray and white, or are red brown with white. Bright yellow eyes.

Female: same as male

Juvenile: lighter gray than adult, may lack the ear tufts

Nest: cavity; former woodpecker cavity; 1 brood per year

Eggs: 4-5; white, unmarked

Incubation: 25-26 days; female incubates, male feeds female during incubation

Fledging: 26-27 days; male and female feed young

Migration: non-migrator

Food: large insects, small mammals, birds, snakes

Compare: The only small owl in the state with ear tufts. Can be gray or rust colored.

Stan's Notes: A common owl active at dusk and during the night. Excellent hearing and eyesight. Seldom gives a screeching call; more commonly gives a tremulous, descending whiny trill that sounds like it came from the sound track of a scary movie. Will nest in wooden nest box. Often seen sunning themselves at nest box holes during winter. Male and female may roost together at night, and are thought to mate for life. Different color phases are called morphs. Gray morph more common than red.

male

female

YEAR-ROUND

American Robin
Turdus migratorius

Size: 9-11" (22.5-28 cm)

Male: Familiar gray bird with rusty red chest, nearly black head and tail, and black streaks on white chin. White eye ring.

Female: similar to male, but has a gray head and duller chest

Juvenile: similar to female, but has speckled chest and brown back

Nest: cup; female builds with help from male; 2 broods per year

Eggs: 4-7; pale blue, unmarked

Incubation: 12-14 days; female incubates

Fledging: 14-16 days; female and male feed young

Migration: complete, to southern states and Central America, small percentage will not migrate

Food: insects, fruit, berries, worms

Compare: Familiar bird to all.

Stan's Notes: Most people don't realize how easy it is to tell the difference between the male and female robin. Look for the male's dark, nearly black head, compared with the female's gray head. Robins are not listening for worms when they cock their heads to one side or the other. They are looking with eyes that are placed far back on the sides of their heads. Small percentage will not migrate, but spend the winter in low swampy areas where they search for leftover berries and insect eggs.

displaying

YEAR-ROUND

NORTHERN MOCKINGBIRD
Mimus polyglottos

Size: 10" (25 cm)

Male: Silvery gray head and back with light gray chest and belly. White wing patches, seen in flight or during display. Tail black with white outer tail feathers. Black bill.

Female: same as male

Juvenile: overall dull gray with a heavily streaked chest, gray bill

Nest: cup; female and male build; 2 broods per year, sometimes more

Eggs: 3-5; blue green with brown markings

Incubation: 12-13 days; female incubates

Fledging: 11-13 days; female and male feed young

Migration: partial migrator in northern states

Food: insects, fruit

Compare: Similar to the Brown Thrasher (pg. 131), but Thrasher is rusty red with a streaked chest. Gray Catbird (pg. 211) is slate gray and lacks Mockingbird's white wing patches. Look for Mockingbird to spread its wings, flash its white wing patches and wag its tail from side to side.

Stan's Notes: Very animated, both male and female perform elaborate mating dances by facing each other, heads and tails erect. They run towards each other, flashing white wing patches, then retreat to nearby cover. Known to imitate other birds, called vocal mimicry, hence its common name. Young males often sing at night.

breeding pg. 37
winter

WINTER

BLACK-BELLIED PLOVER
Pluvialis squatarola

Size: 11-12" (28-30 cm)

Male: Black legs and bill. Winter plumage is light gray with fine streaks on belly. Striking black and white breeding plumage, with a frosty white cap and nape of neck. Black face, neck, chest and sides.

Female: less black on chest and belly than male

Juvenile: grayer than adult, with much less black

Nest: ground; male and female build; 1 brood per year

Eggs: 3-4; pinkish or greenish with black-brown markings

Incubation: 26-27 days; male and female incubate, male during day, female at night

Fledging: 35-45 days; male feeds young, young learn quickly to feed themselves

Migration: complete, to East and Gulf coasts, West Indies to the coast of South America

Food: insects

Compare: Slightly larger than Dunlin (pg. 207) and lacking its long downward-curved bill.

Stan's Notes: Males perform a "butterfly" courtship flight to attract females. Female leaves male and young 12 days after eggs hatch. Breeds at age three. Begins migration in July and August. In flight, in any plumage, Plover displays white rump and stripe on wing with black axillaries (armpit). Often darts across ground to grab an insect and run.

soaring

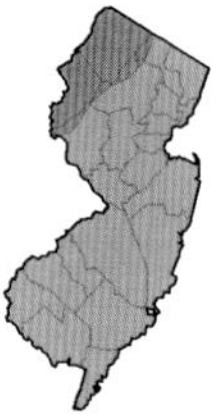

YEAR-ROUND
WINTER

Sharp-shinned Hawk

Accipiter striatus

Size: 10-14" (25-36 cm)

Male: A small woodland hawk with gray brown back and head. Rusty red breast. Long tail with several dark tail bands, widest band at end of squared-off tail. Red eye.

Female: same as male, only larger

Juvenile: same size as adult, with brown back and heavily streaked breast, yellow eye

Nest: platform; female builds; 1 brood per year

Eggs: 4-5; white with brown markings

Incubation: 32-35 days; female incubates

Fledging: 24-27 days; female and male feed young

Migration: complete, to southern states, Mexico and Central America

Food: birds, small mammals

Compare: Nearly identical to Cooper's Hawk (pg. 225), only smaller. Look for squared end of tail on Sharp-shinned, compared with round end of Cooper's.

Stan's Notes: A common hawk of backyards and woodland, they are often seen swooping in on birds visiting feeders. Short rounded wings and long tail allow this hawk to navigate through thick stands of trees in pursuit of prey. Common name comes from the sharp keel on the leading edge of its "shin," although it is actually below rather than above the bird's ankle on the tarsus bone of foot. The tarsus in most birds is round. In flight, head doesn't protrude as far as the head of the Cooper's Hawk.

YEAR-ROUND

Rock Dove
Columba livia

Size: 13" (33 cm)

Male: No set color pattern. Gray to white with patches of iridescent greens and blues, usually with a light rump patch.

Female: same as male

Juvenile: same as adult

Nest: platform; female builds; 3-4 broods per year

Eggs: 1-2; white, unmarked

Incubation: 18-20 days; female and male incubate

Fledging: 25-26 days; female and male feed young

Migration: non-migrator

Food: seeds

Compare: Larger than light-brown-colored Mourning Dove (pg. 139).

Stan's Notes: Also known as Domestic Pigeon, it was introduced to North America from Europe by early settlers. Most common around cities and barnyards, where it scratches for seeds. The wide color variation comes from years of selective breeding while in captivity. Parents feed young a regurgitated liquid called crop-milk the first few days of life. One of the few birds that can drink without tilting its head back. Nests under bridges, on buildings, balconies, barns and sheds. Once poisoned as a "nuisance city bird." Many cities have Peregrine Falcons that feed on Rock Doves, keeping their numbers in check.

soaring

Cooper's Hawk
Accipiter cooperii

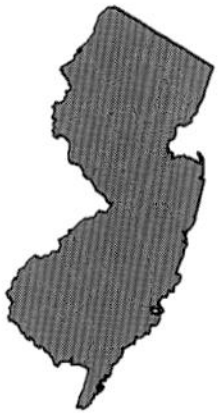

YEAR-ROUND

Size: 14-20" (36-50 cm)

Male: A medium hawk with short wings and a long rounded tail with several black bands. Rusty chest and dark wing tips. Slate gray back. Bright yellow spot at base of gray bill, called a cere. Red eye.

Female: similar to male, only slightly larger

Juvenile: brown back with brown streaks on chest, yellow eye

Nest: platform; male and female build; 1 brood per year

Eggs: 2-4; greenish with brown markings

Incubation: 32-36 days; female and male incubate

Fledging: 28-32 days; male and female feed young

Migration: non-migrator to partial migrator, to southern states and Mexico

Food: small birds, mammals

Compare: Nearly identical to the Sharp-shinned Hawk (pg. 221), only larger, darker gray and with a rounded-off tail.

Stan's Notes: A common hawk of the woodland. In flight, look for its large head, short wings and proportionately long tail. Short stubby wings help it maneuver between trees while pursuing small birds. Will come to feeders, hunting for unaware birds. Flies with long glides followed by a few quick flaps. Known to ambush their prey, they will fly into heavy brush or even run on the ground in pursuit. Nestlings have gray eyes that become bright yellow at one year and later, dark red.

male
female pg. 171

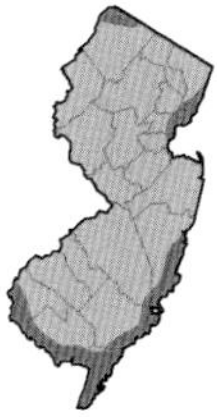

YEAR-ROUND
MIGRATION

Northern Harrier
Circus cyaneus

Size: 24" (60 cm)

Male: A slim, low-flying hawk. Silver gray with large white rump patch and white belly. Faint narrow bands across the tail. Tips of wings black.

Female: dark brown back with brown-streaked breast and belly, large white rump patch, narrow black bands across tail, tips of wings black

Juvenile: similar to female, with orange breast

Nest: platform; female and male build; 1 brood per year

Eggs: 4-8; bluish white, unmarked

Incubation: 31-32 days; female incubates

Fledging: 30-35 days; male and female feed young

Migration: complete, southern states, Central America

Food: mice, snakes

Compare: Slimmer than Red-tailed Hawk (pg. 165). Look for black bands on tail and a white rump patch.

Stan's Notes: One of the easiest hawks to identify. Harriers glide just above ground, following the contours of the land while searching for prey. Wings are held just above the horizontal position, tilting back and forth in the wind, similar to Turkey Vultures. Formerly called Marsh Hawk due to its habit of hunting over marshes. Nests on the ground. At all ages, the Northern Harrier has distinctive owl-like face disks.

Canada Goose
Branta canadensis

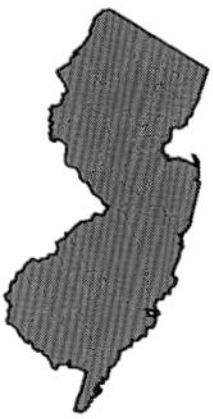

YEAR-ROUND

Size: 25-43" (63-109 cm)

Male: Large gray goose with black neck and head, with a white chin or cheek strap.

Female: same as male

Juvenile: same as adult

Nest: ground; female builds; 1 brood per year

Eggs: 5-10; white, unmarked

Incubation: 25-30 days; female incubates

Fledging: 42-55 days; male and female teach young to feed

Migration: non-migrator to partial migrator, to southern states

Food: aquatic plants, insects, seeds

Compare: A very common bird, hardly ever confused with any other bird.

Stan's Notes: Once not very common, they have adapted to our changed environment very well. Adults will mate for many years, and will only start to breed in their third year. Males often act as sentinels, standing on the edge of the group and bobbing their heads up and down, becoming very aggressive to anyone who approaches. Will hiss as if to display displeasure. Adults molt primary flight feathers while raising young, rendering family groups flightless at the same time. Several subspecies vary geographically around the U. S. Generally they are paler in color in eastern groups, and darker in the western. Their size decreases northward, with the smallest subspecies found on the Arctic tundra.

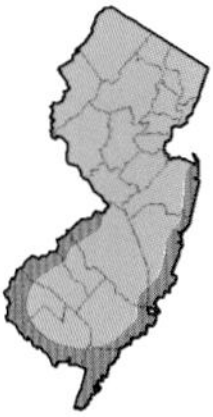

Great Blue Heron
Ardea herodias

Size: 42-52" (107-132 cm)

Male: Tall gray heron with black eyebrow extending into several long plumes off back of head. Long yellow bill. Feathers at base of neck drop down in a kind of necklace.

Female: same as male

Juvenile: same as adult, but more brown than gray, with a black crown and no plumes

Nest: platform; male and female build; 1 brood per year

Eggs: 3-5; blue green, unmarked

Incubation: 27-28 days; female and male incubate

Fledging: 56-60 days; male and female feed young

Migration: complete, to southern states, Central and South Americas

Food: small fish, frogs, insects, snakes

Compare: Similar in size to Great Egret (pg. 275), but the Great Blue Heron is gray and brown, not white.

Stan's Notes: One of the most common herons, it often barks like a dog when startled. Seen stalking small fish in shallow water. Will strike at mice, squirrels and just about anything else it might come across. Flies holding neck in an S shape, with its long legs trailing straight out behind. Wings are held in cupped fashion during flight. Nests in colonies of up to 100 birds. Nests in treetops near or over open water.

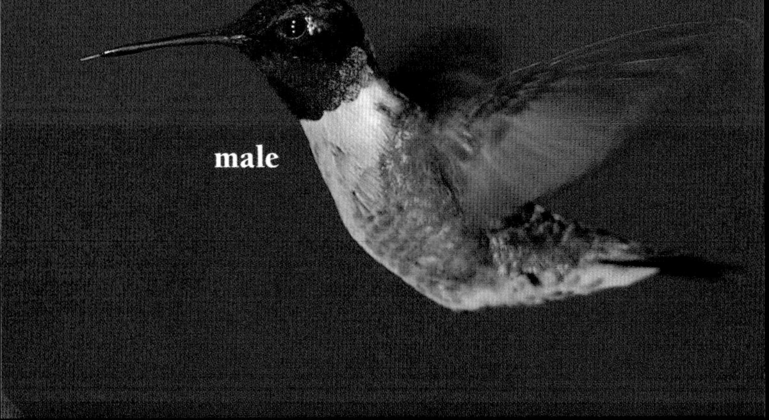
male

female

RUBY-THROATED HUMMINGBIRD
Archilochus colubris

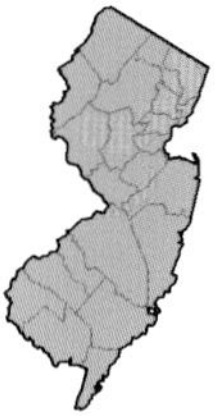

MIGRATION
SUMMER

Size: 3-3½" (7.5-9 cm)

Male: Tiny iridescent green bird with black throat patch that reflects bright ruby red in sunlight.

Female: same as male, lacking throat patch

Juvenile: same as female

Nest: cup; female builds; 1-2 broods per year

Eggs: 2; white, unmarked

Incubation: 12-14 days; female incubates

Fledging: 14-18 days; female feeds young

Migration: complete, to southern states, Mexico and Central America

Food: nectar, insects

Compare: No other bird this small. Sphinx Moth hovers at flowers like the Hummingbird, but has clear wings and a mouth part that looks like a straw, which coils up when not at flower. Moves much slower than Hummingbird and can be approached.

Stan's Notes: Wings create a humming noise, flapping 50 to 60 times per second or faster during chasing flights. Able to hover, fly up and down, and is the only bird to fly backwards. Constructs nest with plant material and spider webs, gluing pieces of lichen on outside of nest for camouflage. Attracted to tubular red flowers. Weighing only two to three grams, it takes about five average-sized hummingbirds to equal the weight of a single chickadee. Heart beats at an incredible 1,260 times a minute and breathes 250 times a minute. Does not sing, but will chatter or buzz to communicate.

male
female pg. 157

WOOD DUCK
Aix sponsa

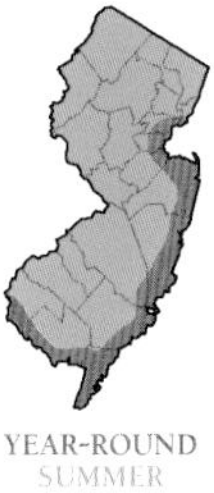

Size: 17-20" (43-50 cm)

Male: A small, highly ornamented dabbling duck with a green head and crest, red eye, and patterned with white and black. Rusty chest and white belly.

Female: brown, similar size and shape to male, has bright white eye ring and not so obvious crest, blue patch on wing often hidden

Juvenile: same as female

Nest: cavity; female lines former woodpecker cavity; 1 brood per year

Eggs: 10-15; creamy white, unmarked

Incubation: 28-36 days; female incubates

Fledging: 56-68 days; female teaches young to feed

Migration: complete, to southern states

Food: aquatic insects, plants, seeds

Compare: Smaller than the male Northern Shoveler (pg. 239). Lacks Shoveler's long wide bill.

Stan's Notes: A common duck of quiet, shallow backwater ponds. Nearly extinct around 1900 due to over-hunting, but doing well now. Nests in old woodpecker holes or nest boxes. Often seen flying deep within a forest or perched high up on branches of trees. Female enters nest cavity from full flight. Females will lay eggs in neighboring female nest, called egg dumping, resulting in some clutches in excess of 20 eggs. Young remain in nest cavity only 24 hours after hatching, then jump from up to 30 feet to the ground or water to follow their mother. After that, they never return to the nest.

Green Heron
Butorides virescens

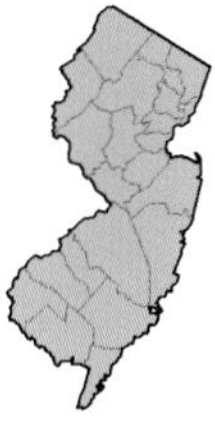

Size: 16-22" (40-56 cm)

Male: A short stocky heron with a blue-green back, and rusty red neck and chest. Dark green crest. Short legs, normally yellow, but turn bright orange during breeding season.

Female: same as male

Juvenile: similar to adult, with blue-gray back and white-streaked chest and neck

Nest: platform; female and male build; 2 broods per year

Eggs: 2-4; light green, unmarked

Incubation: 21-25 days; female and male incubate

Fledging: 35-36 days; female and male feed young

Migration: complete, to South America

Food: fish, insects, aquatic plants

Compare: Much smaller than the Great Blue Heron (pg. 231). Look for a small heron stalking along lakeshore with dark green back.

Stan's Notes: Often gives an explosive rasping "skyew" when startled. Sometimes it looks like it doesn't have a neck, because it holds its head close to its body. Hunts for fish and aquatic insects by waiting along a shore or wades stealthily. Has been known to place an object like an insect on the water surface to attract fish to catch. Has a crest that it raises when excited.

male
female pg. 161

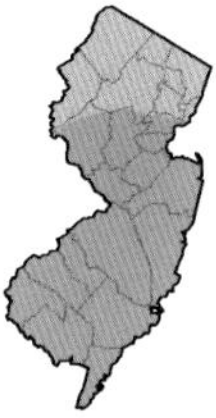

Northern Shoveler
Anas clypeata

Size: 20" (50 cm)

Male: A medium-sized duck with an iridescent green head, rusty sides and a white breast. Has an extraordinarily large spoon-shaped bill, almost always held pointed towards the water.

Female: same spoon-shaped bill, with brown and black all over and blue wing patch

Juvenile: same as female

Nest: ground; female builds; 1 brood per year

Eggs: 9-12; olive, unmarked

Incubation: 22-25 days; female incubates

Fledging: 30-60 days; female leads young to food

Migration: complete, to southern states and Central America

Food: aquatic insects, plants

Compare: Similar to the male Mallard (pg. 243), but Shoveler has a large, characteristic spoon-shaped bill. Larger than the average male Wood Duck (pg. 235) and lacks the Wood Duck's crest.

Stan's Notes: Seen in small flocks of five to ten, swimming low in water with large bills always pointed towards water, as if they're too heavy to lift. More commonly seen during spring migration. Feeds primarily by filtering tiny plants and insects from the water's surface with bill.

female pg. 261
male

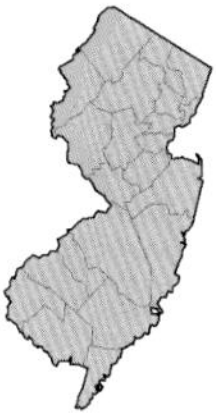

MIGRATION
SUMMER

Common Merganser
Mergus merganser

Size: 27" (69 cm)

Male: A long, thin, duck-like bird with a green head and black back. White sides, chest and neck. Long pointed bill.

Female: same size and shape as male, but with a rust red head, ragged "hair" on crest, gray body, white chest and long pointed bill

Juvenile: same as female

Nest: cavity; female lines former woodpecker cavity; 1 brood per year

Eggs: 9-11; ivory without markings

Incubation: 28-33 days; female incubates

Fledging: 70-80 days; female feeds young

Migration: complete, to southern states, Central America and Mexico

Food: fish, aquatic insects

Compare: Male Hooded Merganser (pg. 43) has white patch on head and rusty brown sides.

Stan's Notes: Mergansers are shallow water divers that feed on small fish in no more than 10 or 15 feet of water. More commonly seen along rivers than lakes. Their bills have a fine serrated-like edge to help catch slippery fish. Females often lay eggs in other merganser nests, called egg dumping, resulting in broods of up to 15 young per mother. The male leaves the female as soon as she starts to incubate eggs. Young that lose their mothers will be accepted by other merganser mothers with young.

female pg. 173
male

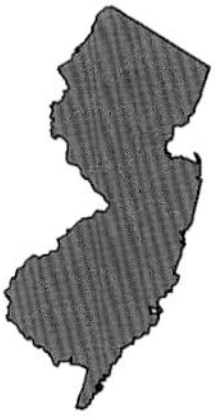
YEAR-ROUND

MALLARD
Anas platyrhynchos

Size: 27-28" (69-71 cm)

Male: Large, bulbous green head, white necklace and rust brown or chestnut-colored chest. Combination of gray and white on sides. Yellow bill, legs and feet.

Female: all-brown duck with orange and black bill and small blue and white wing mark, called a speculum

Juvenile: same as female, but with yellow bill

Nest: ground; female builds; 1 brood per year

Eggs: 7-10; greenish to whitish, unmarked

Incubation: 26-30 days; female incubates

Fledging: 42-52 days; female leads young to food

Migration: complete, to southern states, small percentage non-migrator

Food: seeds, plants, aquatic insects, ground feeders offering corn

Compare: The male Northern Shoveler (pg. 239) has a white chest with rust on sides and dark spoon-shaped bill.

Stan's Notes: Familiar duck of lakes and ponds. Will return to place of birth. The name "Mallard" comes from the Latin *masculus*, meaning "male," referring to the habit of males not taking part in raising ducklings. Both male and female have white tails and white underwings. Black central tail feathers of male curl upward.

male
female pg. 281

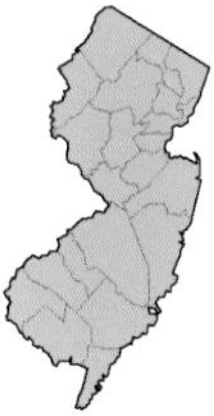

American Redstart
Setophaga ruticilla

Size: 5" (13 cm)

Male: A small, striking black bird with contrasting patches of orange on sides, wings and tail. White belly.

Female: olive brown with yellow patches instead of the male's orange, white belly

Juvenile: same as female, immature males tinged orange for first year

Nest: cup; female builds; 1 brood per year

Eggs: 3-5; off-white with brown markings

Incubation: 12 days; female incubates

Fledging: 9 days; female and male feed young

Migration: complete, to Mexico, Central and South Americas

Food: insects, seeds, berries rarely

Compare: The male Red-winged Blackbird (pg. 9) and the male Baltimore Oriole (pg. 247) are considerably larger, at roughly eight inches. Only small black and orange bird flitting around tops of trees.

Stan's Notes: A common and widespread warbler in New Jersey. Prefers large unbroken tracts of forest. Appears to be hyperactive when feeding, hovering, and darting back and forth to glean insects from leaves. Look for flashing black and orange color high in the trees. They often droop wings and fan tails just before launching out to catch an insect.

male
female pg. 295

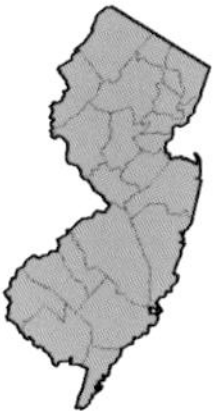
SUMMER

BALTIMORE ORIOLE
Icterus galbula

Size: 7-8" (18-20 cm)

Male: Bright, flaming orange bird with black head and black extending down nape of neck onto the back. Black wings with white and orange wing bars. Orange tail with black streaks. Gray bill and dark eye.

Female: pale yellow bird with gray brown wings, white wing bars, gray bill and dark eye

Juvenile: same as female

Nest: pendulous; female builds; 1 brood per year

Eggs: 4-5; bluish with brown markings

Incubation: 12-14 days; female incubates

Fledging: 12-14 days; female and male feed young

Migration: complete, to Mexico, Central and South Americas

Food: insects, fruit, nectar, will come to orange halves and nectar feeders

Compare: The male Orchard Oriole (pg. 249) is much darker orange than the Baltimore's flaming orange. Male American Redstart (pg. 245) is smaller and has more black than orange.

Stan's Notes: Fantastic songsters, these birds are often heard before seen. Easily attracted to a feeder offering grape jelly, orange halves or sugar water (nectar). Parents bring young to feeders. They build their sock-like nest at the outermost branches of tall trees. They often return to the same area year after year. Some of the last birds to arrive in spring (May) and first to leave in fall (September). They sit in the tops of the trees feeding on caterpillars.

female pg. 297
male

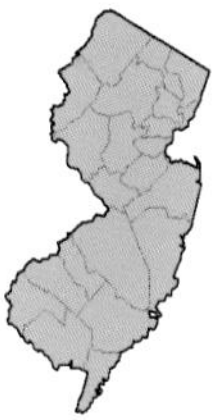

SUMMER

ORCHARD ORIOLE
Icterus spurius

Size: 7-8" (18-20 cm)

Male: Dull orange bird with black head and black extending down the back. Black chin, wings and tail. A single white wing bar. Long, thin black bill with a small gray mark on lower mandible (jaw).

Female: olive green back with a dull yellow belly, two white wing bars on dark gray wings

Juvenile: same as female

Nest: pendulous; female builds; 1 brood per year

Eggs: 3-5; pale blue to white with brown markings

Incubation: 11-12 days; female and male incubate

Fledging: 11-14 days; female and male feed young

Migration: complete, to central Mexico and northern South America

Food: insects, fruit, comes to fruit/nectar feeders

Compare: Similar to male Baltimore Oriole (pg. 247), but the male Orchard Oriole has a much darker orange body.

Stan's Notes: Prefers open woods and orchards, hence its common name. They eat insects until wild fruits start to ripen. One of the last birds to arrive in spring and one of the first to leave each fall, spending only about three to four months in New Jersey. Usually nests alone, but sometimes in small colonies. Parents bring young to jelly and orange half feeders shortly after fledging. Many people mistakenly think the orioles have left during the summer, but in fact, the birds are concentrating on finding insects to feed their young.

female pg. 83
male

House Finch
Carpodacus mexicanus

YEAR-ROUND

Size: 5" (13 cm)

Male: Orange red face, chest and rump, with a dark marking behind eye. Brown wings streaked with white. A white belly with brown streaks. Brown cap.

Female: brown with heavily streaked white chest

Juvenile: similar to female

Nest: cup, sometimes in cavities; female builds; 2 broods per year

Eggs: 4-5; pale blue, lightly marked

Incubation: 12-14 days; female incubates

Fledging: 15-19 days; female and male feed young

Migration: non-migrator to partial migrator, moves around to find food

Food: seeds, fruit, leaf buds, will come to seed feeders

Compare: Very similar to male Purple Finch (pg. 253), lacking the Purple Finch's red cap. Look for the streaked chest and belly, and brown cap of male House Finch.

Stan's Notes: The House Finch was originally introduced to Long Island, New York, in the 1940s from western America. A very social bird, it visits feeders in small flocks. Seems to prefer nesting in hanging flower baskets. Incubating female is fed by male. Loud and cheerful warbling song.

female pg. 97
male

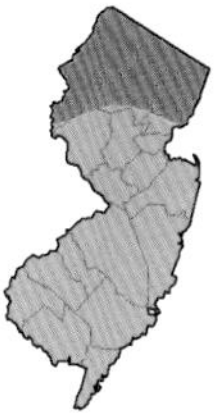

Purple Finch

Carpodacus purpureus

Size: 6" (15 cm)

Male: Raspberry red head, cap, breast, back and rump. Brownish wings and tail.

Female: heavily streaked brown and white with a large white eye line

Juvenile: same as female

Nest: cup; female and male build; 1 brood per year

Eggs: 4-5; greenish blue with brown markings

Incubation: 12-13 days; female incubates

Fledging: 13-14 days; female and male feed young

Migration: irruptive, moves around the state to find food

Food: seeds, insects, fruit, will come to seed feeders

Compare: Redder than the orange red male House Finch (pg. 251), with a clear (no streaking) red breast. The male House Finch has a brown cap, compared with the male Purple Finch's red cap.

Stan's Notes: Year-round resident of northern New Jersey. Travels in flocks of up to 50. Comes to seed feeders along with House Finches, making it hard to tell them apart. A rich loud song and a distinctive "tic" note is made only in flight. Not a purple color, the Latin name *purpureus* means "crimson" or other reddish color.

female
pg. 293
male

Scarlet Tanager
Piranga olivacea

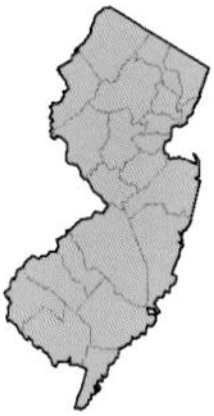

SUMMER

Size: 7" (18 cm)

Male: Bright scarlet red bird with jet black wings and tail. Ivory bill and dark eye.

Female: drab greenish yellow with olive wings and tail, whitish wing linings, dark eye

Juvenile: same as female

Nest: platform; female builds; 1 brood per year

Eggs: 4-5; blue green with brown markings

Incubation: 13-14 days; female incubates

Fledging: 9-11 days; female and male feed young

Migration: complete, to Central and South Americas

Food: insects, fruit

Compare: The male Northern Cardinal (pg. 257) has black mask and red bill, and lacks the black wings of the male Scarlet Tanager.

Stan's Notes: Male sheds (molts) its bright red plumage in the fall, appearing more like the female. Prefers mature unbroken woodland, where it hunts for insects high in the tops of trees. Requires a minimum of four acres for nesting; prefers eight acres. Tropical-looking birds, they arrive late in spring and leave early in autumn. Scarlet Tanager is included in some 240 tanager species in the world. Nearly all are brightly colored and live in the tropics. The name "Tanager" comes from a South American Tupi Indian word meaning "any small, brightly colored bird."

female pg. 123
male

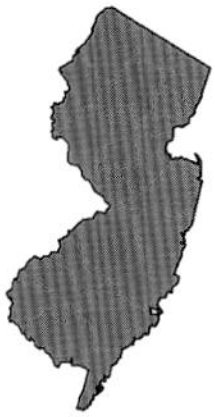

YEAR-ROUND

Northern Cardinal
Cardinalis cardinalis

Size: 8-9" (20-22.5 cm)

Male: All-red bird with a black mask extending from face down to chin and throat. Large red bill and crest.

Female: buff brown with tinges of red on crest and wings, same black mask and red bill

Juvenile: same as female, with blackish gray bill

Nest: cup; female builds; 2-3 broods per year

Eggs: 3-4; bluish white with brown markings

Incubation: 12-13 days; female and male incubate

Fledging: 9-10 days; female and male feed young

Migration: non-migrator

Food: seeds, insects, fruit, will come to seed feeders

Compare: The male Scarlet Tanager (pg. 255) has black wings and tail.

Stan's Notes: A familiar backyard bird. Look for male feeding female during courtship. Male feeds young of first brood by himself while female builds second nest. Their name comes from the Latin word *cardinalis*, which means "important." Very territorial during spring, it will fight its own reflection in a window. Non-territorial in winter, they gather in small flocks of up to 20 birds. Both male and female sing, and can be heard anytime of year. Listen for their "whata-cheer-cheer-cheer" territorial call in spring.

female pg. 209

WINTER

Pine Grosbeak

Pinicola enucleator

Size: 9" (22.5 cm)

Male: A plump, rosy red and gray winter finch with a long dark tail. Dark wings have a smattering of gray and two white wing bars. Short, stubby, dark pointed bill.

Female: mostly gray with dark wings and tail, head and rump tinged dull yellow

Juvenile: male juvenile has touch of red on head and rump, female juvenile similar to adult

Nest: cup; female builds; 1 brood per year

Eggs: 4-5, bluish green, unmarked

Incubation: 13-15 days, female incubates

Fledging: 13-20 days, female and male feed young

Migration: non-migrator to irruptive, moves around to find food

Food: seeds, fruit, insects, will come to feeders

Compare: Much larger than the male Purple Finch (pg. 253) and male House Finch (pg. 251).

Stan's Notes: A winter finch throughout northern New Jersey in some years, and not so common in others. Often seen along roads or on the ground eating tiny grains of sand and dirt to aid in digestion. A seed eater that favors conifer woods, but also moves into deciduous woods where it relishes ash tree seeds. Flies with typical finch-like undulating pattern while calling a soft whistle. During breeding season both male and female develop a pouch in bottom of mouth to transport seeds to young. Very tame and approachable bird. Often seen bathing in fluffy snow.

male pg. 241
female

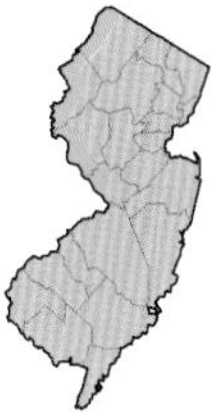

Common Merganser
Mergus merganser

Size: 27" (69 cm)

Female: A long, thin, duck-like bird with a rust red head and ragged "hair" on back of head. Gray body. White chest. Long pointed bill.

Male: same size and shape as female, but with a green head, black back, white sides, chest and neck, and long pointed bill

Juvenile: same as female

Nest: cavity; female lines former woodpecker cavity; 1 brood per year

Eggs: 9-11; ivory without markings

Incubation: 28-33 days; female incubates

Fledging: 70-80 days; female feeds young

Migration: complete, to southern states, Central America and Mexico

Food: fish, aquatic insects

Compare: Female Hooded Merganser (pg. 153) has similar shape, but is much smaller with a brownish red head.

Stan's Notes: Mergansers are shallow water divers that feed on small fish in no more than 10 or 15 feet of water. More commonly seen along rivers than lakes. Their bills have a fine serrated-like edge to help catch slippery fish. Females often lay eggs in other merganser nests, called egg dumping, resulting in broods of up to 15 young per mother. The male leaves the female as soon as she starts to incubate eggs. Young that lose their mothers will be accepted by other merganser mothers with young.

Forster's Tern
Sterna forsteri

Size: 14-15" (36-38 cm)

Male: A white and gray tern with jet black crown, and an orange bill with a black tip. Leading edge of wings is gray, trailing edge is white. Characteristic forked tail is long and white.

Female: same as male

Juvenile: similar to adult, minus the black crown

Nest: platform; female and male build; 1 brood per year

Eggs: 3-5; tan to white with brown markings

Incubation: 23-24 days; female and male incubate

Fledging: 24-26 days; male and female feed young

Migration: complete, to Central America

Food: small fish, aquatic insects

Compare: Similar to other terns. Look for a jet black crown, orange bill with black tip and white tips of wings.

Stan's Notes: Usually seen in small colonies. Catches small fish by diving into water head-first. Will catch insects in flight. Named after Johann Reinhold Forster, a German naturalist who accompanied Captain Cook around the world in 1772. Builds platform nest on floating vegetation. Nests in small colonies in shallow water marshes.

winter
breeding

Laughing Gull
Larus atricilla

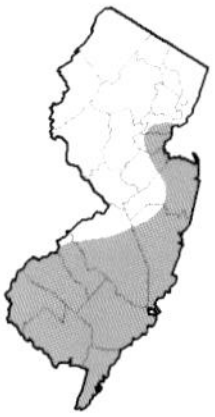

SUMMER

Size: 16-17" (40-43 cm); up to 3⅓-foot wingspan

Male: Adult breeding plumage of black head "hood," white neck, chest and belly. Slate gray back and wings with black wing tips. Orange bill. Winter plumage has no "hood" and has a black bill.

Female: same as male

Juvenile: brown throughout, gray sides, lacking the black head and white chest, gray bill

Nest: ground; male and female build; 1 brood per year

Eggs: 2-4; olive with brown markings

Incubation: 18-20 days; female and male incubate

Fledging: 30-35 days; male and female feed young

Migration: complete, to East and Gulf coasts, Central and South Americas

Food: fish, insects, aquatic insects

Compare: Smaller than the Ring-billed Gull (pg. 267) and Herring Gull (pg. 271). Look for black head "hood," and slate gray back and wings of Laughing Gull.

Stan's Notes: A "three-year" gull, Laughing Gull starts out mostly brown and gray. Second year it resembles the adult version, but lacks complete black head "hood." Third year is breeding plumage. Nests in marshes in large colonies. Male tosses his head back and calls to attract a mate. Nest is a scrape on ground lined with grass, sticks and rocks. Young fed a half-digested regurgitant by adults.

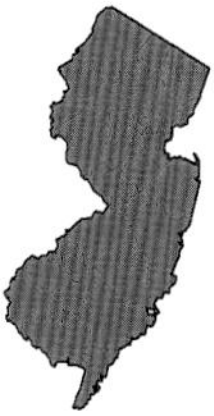

YEAR-ROUND

Ring-billed Gull
Larus delawarensis

Size: 19" (48 cm)

Male: White bird with gray wings, black wing tips spotted with white, and white tail seen in flight. Yellow bill with a black ring near tip. Yellowish legs and feet.

Female: same as male

Juvenile: mostly gray version of adult, with a dark band at end of tail

Nest: ground; female and male build; 1 brood per year

Eggs: 2-4; off-white with brown markings

Incubation: 20-21 days; female and male incubate

Fledging: 20-40 days; female and male feed young

Migration: complete, to southern states and Mexico

Food: insects, fish, scavenges

Compare: Similar to Herring Gull (pg. 271), which has an orange mark on tip of lower bill. Herring Gull has pink legs and feet, and lacks Ring-billed Gull's black ring.

Stan's Notes: This is the common gull of garbage dumps and parking lots. They are expanding their range and remain farther north longer due to successful scavenging in cities. They acquire a new and different plumage in each of the first three autumns and don't attain adult plumage until third year. They attain ring on bill after first winter.

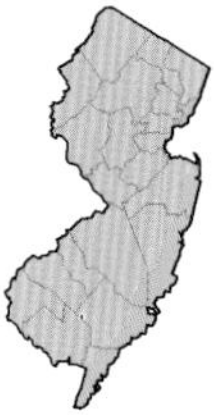

SUMMER

Snowy Egret
Egretta thula

Size: 24" (60 cm)

Male: An all-white bird with black bill and legs. Bright yellow feet and eyes. Long feather plumes on head, neck and back during breeding season.

Female: same as male

Juvenile: similar to adult, but lacks the plumes and backs of legs are yellow

Nest: platform; female and male build; 1 brood per year

Eggs: 3-5; light blue-green, unmarked

Incubation: 20-24 days; female and male incubate

Fledging: 28-30 days; female and male feed young

Migration: complete, to Gulf coast and Mexico

Food: aquatic insects, fish

Compare: Very similar to the Great Egret (pg. 275), only smaller with yellow feet and black bill.

Stan's Notes: Now common in wetlands, they were once eliminated (extirpated) from New Jersey by the end of 1800s due to unregulated hunting. Returned to New Jersey in 1928. Colonies may include up to several hundred nests. Nests are low in shrubs five to ten feet tall or are on the ground, usually mixed amongst other egret and heron nests. Chicks hatch days apart (asynchronous), leading to starvation of the last to hatch. Will actively "hunt" prey by moving around quickly, stirring up small fish and aquatic insects with its feet. In breeding state, a yellow patch at base of bill and yellow feet turn orange-red.

Herring Gull
Larus argentatus

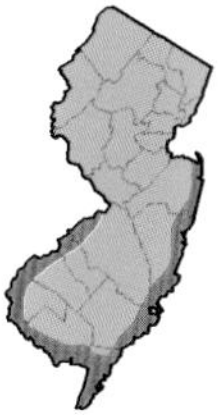

YEAR-ROUND
SUMMER

Size: 23-26" (58-66 cm)

Male: Common "sea gull" of large lakes. A snow-white bird with slate gray wings and black wing tips with tiny white spots. Yellow bill with red spot near tip of lower mandible. Pinkish legs.

Female: same as male

Juvenile: uniformly mottled brown to gray, black bill

Nest: ground; female and male build; 1 brood per year

Eggs: 2-3; olive with brown markings

Incubation: 24-28 days; female and male incubate

Fledging: 35-36 days; female and male feed young

Migration: complete, to coasts that remain unfrozen in North America

Food: fish, insects, clams, eggs, baby birds

Compare: Larger than Ring-billed Gull (pg. 267), which has a black ring around its bill and lacks orange dot on lower mandible. Ring-billed Gull has yellow legs, compared with the Herring Gull's pinkish legs.

Stan's Notes: An opportunistic bird, scavenging for food from dumpsters, but will also take other birds' eggs and young right from nest. Often drops clams and other shellfish from heights to break shells and get to the soft interior. Nests in colonies, returning to same site year after year. Lines nest with grasses and seaweed. Adults molt to a dirty gray in winter, looking similar to juveniles. Takes about four years for juveniles to obtain adult plumage.

blue morph
white morph

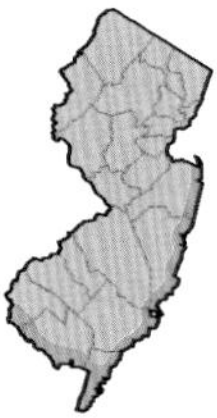

MIGRATION
WINTER

Snow Goose
Chen caerulescens

Size: 25-38" (63-96 cm)

Male: A mostly white goose with varying patches of black and brown. Black wing tips and pink bill and legs.

Female: same as male

Juvenile: overall dull gray with dark bill

Nest: ground; female builds; 1 brood per year

Eggs: 3-5; white, unmarked

Incubation: 23-25 days; female incubates

Fledging: 45-49 days; female and male teach young to feed

Migration: complete, to East coast, southern states and Mexico

Food: aquatic insects and plants

Compare: The Mute Swan (pg. 279) is nearly twice the average size of Snow Goose and lacks the black wing tips of Snow Goose. Much smaller than Tundra Swan (pg. 277), lacking Tundra's black bill and legs. Smaller than the Canada Goose (pg. 229), lacking black neck and white chin strap.

Stan's Notes: Often seen in large flocks and by the thousands each winter along the Delaware Bay. Two color types, called phases or morphs. Gray phase is often called blue, with a white head, pink bill and legs, and gray chest and back. The other is pure white with black wing tips. Breeds in large colonies on the tundra of northern Canada. Females don't breed until ages two to three. Older females produce more eggs and have more success than younger females.

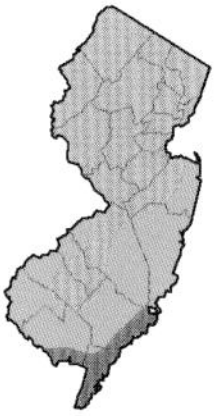

Great Egret
Ardea alba

Size: 38" (96 cm)

Male: Tall, thin, elegant all-white bird with long, pointed yellow bill. Black stilt-like legs. Black feet.

Female: same as male

Juvenile: same as adult

Nest: platform; male and female build; 1 brood per year

Eggs: 2-3; light blue, unmarked

Incubation: 23-26 days; female and male incubate

Fledging: 43-49 days; female and male feed young

Migration: complete, to southern states, Mexico and Central America

Food: fish, aquatic insects, frogs, crayfish

Compare: Smaller in size and similar in shape to Great Blue Heron (pg. 231).

Stan's Notes: A tall and stately bird, the Great Egret slowly stalks shallow wetlands looking for small fish to spear with its long sharp bill. Nests in colonies of up to 100 birds. Now protected, they were hunted to near extinction for their long white plumage. The name "Egret" came from the French word *aigrette*, which means "ornamental tufts of plumes." The plumes are grown near the tail during breeding season.

MIGRATION
WINTER

TUNDRA SWAN
Cygnus columbianus

Size: 50-54" (127-137 cm)

Male: Large all-white swan with all-black bill, legs and feet. Has a small yellow mark in front of eye.

Female: same as male

Juvenile: same size as adult, gray plumage and pinkish gray bill

Nest: ground; female and male build; 1 brood per year

Eggs: 4-5; creamy white, unmarked

Incubation: 35-40 days; female and male incubate

Fledging: 60-70 days; female and male feed young

Migration: complete, to East coast near Chesapeake Bay

Food: plants, aquatic insects

Compare: Mute Swan (pg. 279) is slightly larger and has an orange bill with a prominent knob near the face.

Stan's Notes: Nests on the tundra of northern Canada and Alaska, hence its common name. Migrates diagonally across North America to reach wintering grounds along the East coast. Often seen in large family groups of up to 20 individuals. The young are easy to distinguish by their overall gray color. Gives a high-pitched whistle-like call. Usually only seen during the spring and fall migrations. Gathers in large numbers in some lakes and rivers to rest, usually staying until the water freezes before continuing the migration. Flies in large V-shaped wedges.

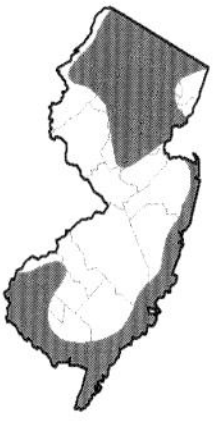

Mute Swan
Cygnus olor

Size: 60" (152 cm)

Male: All white with prominent black knob at base of a large orange bill. Holds neck in an S shape with bill pointed towards the surface of the water.

Female: same as male

Juvenile: brown to gray, gray bill with black base lacks the prominent knob

Nest: ground; female and male build; 1 brood per year

Eggs: 4-8; light gray, lacking any markings

Incubation: 35-40 days; female incubates with help from male

Fledging: 115-150 days; female and male feed young

Migration: partial migrator, moves to areas with open water during winter

Food: aquatic insects and plants

Compare: Very similar to Tundra Swan (pg. 277), but has an orange bill with a prominent knob near the face.

Stan's Notes: An introduced species usually found in parks, zoos and golf courses is now found in the wild. Often swims with wings held arched over its back. Its neck is always held in an S shape. Tundra Swan lacks these features. Can be an aggressive bird, giving a loud hiss when disturbed or threatened.

female
male pg. 245

AMERICAN REDSTART
Setophaga ruticilla

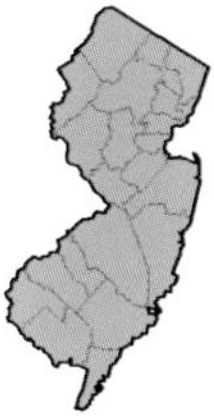

Size: 5" (13 cm)

Female: Olive brown with yellow patches on sides, wings and tail. White belly.

Male: small, striking black bird with contrasting patches of orange on sides, wings and tail, white belly

Juvenile: same as female, immature males tinged orange for first year

Nest: cup; female builds; 1 brood per year

Eggs: 3-5; off-white with brown markings

Incubation: 12 days; female incubates

Fledging: 9 days; female and male feed young

Migration: complete, to Mexico, Central and South Americas

Food: insects, seeds, berries rarely

Compare: Similar to female Yellow-rumped Warbler (pg. 189), but lacking the Warbler's yellow patch on rump.

Stan's Notes: A common and widespread warbler in New Jersey. Prefers large unbroken tracts of forest. Appears to be hyperactive when feeding, hovering, and darting back and forth to glean insects from leaves. Look for flashing black and orange color high in the trees. They often droop wings and fan tails just before launching out to catch an insect.

male

female

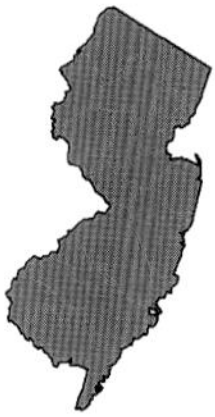

YEAR-ROUND

AMERICAN GOLDFINCH
Carduelis tristis

Size: 5" (13 cm)

Male: A perky yellow bird with a black patch on forehead. Black tail with conspicuous white rump. Black wings with white wing bars. No marking on the chest. Dramatic change in color during winter, similar to female.

Female: dull olive yellow without a black crown, brown black wings and white rump

Juvenile: same as female

Nest: cup; female builds; 1 brood per year

Eggs: 4-6; pale blue, unmarked

Incubation: 10-12 days; female incubates

Fledging: 11-17 days; female and male feed young

Migration: partial migrator, moves around North America in flocks of up to 20

Food: seeds, insects, will come to seed feeders

Compare: Confused with other winter birds. The Pine Siskin (pg. 87) has streaked chest and belly, and yellow wing bars. Female Purple Finch (pg. 97) has heavily streaked chest and white line above eye. Female House Finch (pg. 83) has a heavily streaked white chest.

Stan's Notes: Often called Wild Canary. Feeder bird that enjoys Nyger Thistle. Late summer nesting, uses silky down from wild thistle for nest. Appears roller-coaster-like in flight. Listen for them to twitter during flight. Almost always in small flocks. Moves only far enough south to find food. Small percentage stays all winter.

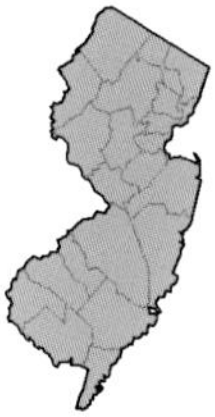

SUMMER

Common Yellowthroat
Geothlypis trichas

Size: 5" (13 cm)

Male: An olive brown bird with a bright yellow throat and breast, and a white belly. Distinctive black mask outlined in white. Long, thin, pointed black bill.

Female: same as male, only lacking black mask

Juvenile: same as female

Nest: cup; female builds; 2 broods per year

Eggs: 3-5; white with brown markings

Incubation: 11-12 days; female incubates

Fledging: 10-11 days; female and male feed young

Migration: complete, to southern states and Central America

Food: insects

Compare: Found in similar habitat as the American Goldfinch (pg. 283), but lacks the male's black crown and wing bars. Male Yellow Warbler (pg. 289) has fine orange streaks on chest and lacks black mask. Yellow-rumped Warbler (pg. 189) only has spots of yellow, compared with Yellowthroat's yellow breast.

Stan's Notes: A common warbler of open fields and marshes. A frequent cowbird host. Young remain dependent upon parents longer than most warblers. It has a cheerful, well-known song, "witchity-witchity-witchity-witchity." Males perform a curious courtship display, bouncing in and out of tall grass while uttering an unusual song.

male

female

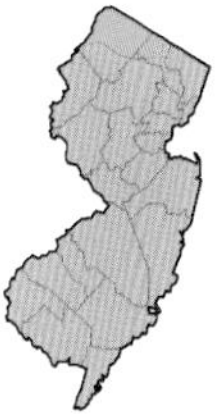

MIGRATION SUMMER

Magnolia Warbler
Dendroica magnolia

Size: 5" (13 cm)

Male: A yellow and black warbler with a white eyebrow and gray crown. White wing patch and yellow rump with obvious white patches on tail. Heavy black streaks on chest.

Female: similar to male, lacks black on face, has two white wing bars

Juvenile: same as female

Nest: cup; female and male build; 1 brood per year

Eggs: 3-5; white with brown markings

Incubation: 11-13 days; female incubates

Fledging: 8-10 days; female and male feed young

Migration: complete, to Central America

Food: insects

Compare: More yellow than Yellow-rumped Warbler (pg. 189). Look for the yellow chest and belly with heavy black streaks. The Yellow Warbler (pg. 289) lacks black back and face. Prairie Warbler (pg. 291) has olive back with chestnut-colored streaks.

Stan's Notes: A common warbler in New Jersey during spring migration. Look for them low in trees, where they feed on insects. Often fan their tails while picking insects from the underside of leaves. Males often feed higher up in trees than females. Nests throughout Canada and northern states. Named by chance when ornithologist Alexander Wilson spotted the bird in a magnolia tree. Has been able to adapt to second growth forest, so its populations are stable.

male

female

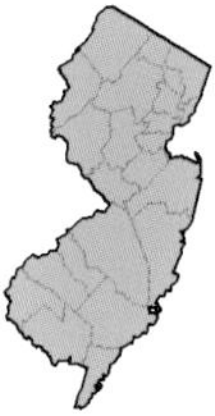

SUMMER

YELLOW WARBLER
Dendroica petechia

Size: 5" (13 cm)

Male: Yellow warbler with orange streaks on the chest and belly. Long, pointed dark bill.

Female: same as male, lacking orange streaking

Juvenile: similar to adult, only much duller

Nest: cup; female builds; 1 brood per year

Eggs: 4-5; white with brown markings

Incubation: 11-12 days; female incubates

Fledging: 10-12 days; female and male feed young

Migration: complete, to southern states, Mexico, Central and South Americas

Food: insects

Compare: Look for orange streaking on chest of male. The male American Goldfinch (pg. 283) has black wings and cap. The female Yellow Warbler is similar to the female American Goldfinch (pg. 283), but lacks its white wing bars.

Stan's Notes: A common warbler of gardens and shrubby areas not far from water. Males are often seen higher up in trees than females. Females are less conspicuous. Starts to migrate south in July and is complete in August. Migrates at night in mixed flocks of other warblers. Rests and feeds during the day.

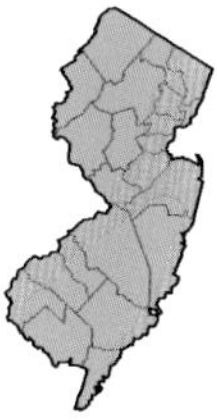

MIGRATION
SUMMER

PRAIRIE WARBLER
Dendroica discolor

Size: 5" (13 cm)

Male: Olive back with chestnut-colored streaks. Bright yellow from the chin to belly. Black streaks on sides from the neck down. Black line through eye. Yellow eyebrow.

Female: same as male, only duller

Juvenile: similar to female

Nest: cup; female builds; 2 broods per year

Eggs: 3-5; white with brown markings

Incubation: 11-14 days; female incubates

Fledging: 8-11 days; female and male feed young

Migration: complete, to Caribbean

Food: insects

Compare: More black than Yellow Warbler (pg. 289) and less black than the Magnolia Warbler (pg. 287). Lacks the complete black mask of the Common Yellowthroat (pg. 285). Watch for the Prairie Warbler to twitch its tail when feeding.

Stan's Notes: A very common and widespread warbler in New Jersey. Nests in dry, brushy clearings and forest edges, thus making it a perfect host for the Brown-headed Cowbird. Will sometimes desert a parasitized nest. Has greatly expanded its range in New Jersey over the past 30 years, now nesting throughout the state. Prairie Warblers return to New Jersey in late April to mid-May in mixed flocks of warblers. Nests in upright fork of trees. Feeds young mainly caterpillars. Unfortunately, it was misnamed when it was first found in a barren area in Kentucky.

female
male pg. 255

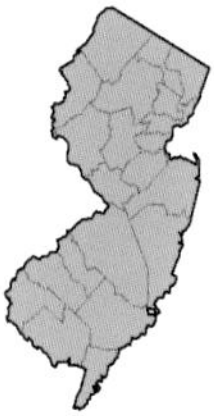

SUMMER

Scarlet Tanager
Piranga olivacea

Size: 7" (18 cm)

Female: Drab greenish yellow with olive wings and tail. Whitish wing linings. Dark eye.

Male: bright scarlet red bird with jet black wings and tail, ivory bill and dark eye

Juvenile: same as female

Nest: platform; female builds; 1 brood per year

Eggs: 4-5; blue green with brown markings

Incubation: 13-14 days; female incubates

Fledging: 9-11 days; female and male feed young

Migration: complete, to Central and South Americas

Food: insects, fruit

Compare: Female Northern Cardinal (pg. 123) has black mask and red bill, but lacks the dark wings of the female Scarlet Tanager. Larger than female American Goldfinch (pg. 283) and lacks the Goldfinch's white wing bars. Female Baltimore Oriole (pg. 295) has gray brown wings and white wing bars.

Stan's Notes: Male sheds (molts) its bright red plumage in the fall, appearing more like the female. Prefers mature unbroken woodland, where it hunts for insects high in the tops of trees. Requires a minimum of four acres for nesting; prefers eight acres. Tropical-looking birds, they arrive late in spring and leave early in autumn. Scarlet Tanager is included in some 240 tanager species in the world. Nearly all are brightly colored and live in the tropics. The name "Tanager" comes from a South American Tupi Indian word meaning "any small, brightly colored bird."

male pg. 247
female

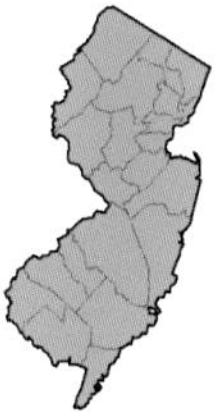
SUMMER

Baltimore Oriole
Icterus galbula

Size: 7-8" (18-20 cm)

Female: Pale yellow bird with gray brown wings, white wing bars. Gray bill and dark eye.

Male: bright, flaming orange bird with black head and black extending down nape of neck onto back, black wings with white and orange wing bars, orange tail with black streaks, gray bill and dark eye

Juvenile: same as female

Nest: pendulous; female builds; 1 brood per year

Eggs: 4-5; bluish with brown markings

Incubation: 12-14 days; female incubates

Fledging: 12-14 days; female and male feed young

Migration: complete, to Mexico, Central and South Americas

Food: insects, fruit, nectar, will come to orange halves and nectar feeders

Compare: The female Oriole is often confused with female Scarlet Tanager (pg. 293), which has olive-colored wings.

Stan's Notes: Fantastic songsters, these birds are often heard before seen. Easily attracted to a feeder offering grape jelly, orange halves or sugar water (nectar). Parents bring young to feeders. They build their sock-like nest at the outermost branches of tall trees. They often return to the same area year after year. Some of the last birds to arrive in spring (May) and first to leave in fall (September). They sit in the tops of the trees feeding on caterpillars.

male pg. 249
female

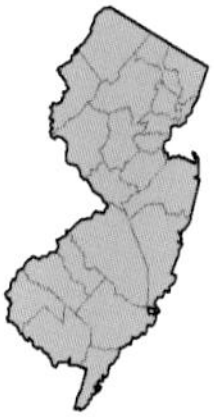

SUMMER

ORCHARD ORIOLE
Icterus spurius

Size: 7-8" (18-20 cm)

Female: An olive green bird with a dull yellow belly, two white wing bars on dark gray wings. Long, thin black bill with a small gray mark on lower mandible (jaw).

Male: dull orange with a black head, chin, upper back, wings and tail, single white wing bar

Juvenile: same as female

Nest: pendulous; female builds; 1 brood per year

Eggs: 3-5; pale blue to white with brown markings

Incubation: 11-12 days; female and male incubate

Fledging: 11-14 days; female and male feed young

Migration: complete, to central Mexico and northern South America

Food: insects, fruit, comes to fruit/nectar feeders

Compare: Similar to female Baltimore Oriole (pg. 295), which has a brighter yellow belly, and female Scarlet Tanager (pg. 293), which has olive-colored wings.

Stan's Notes: Prefers open woods and orchards, hence its common name. They eat insects until wild fruits start to ripen. One of the last birds to arrive in spring and one of the first to leave each fall, spending only about three to four months in New Jersey. Usually nests alone, but sometimes in small colonies. Parents bring young to jelly and orange half feeders shortly after fledging. Many people mistakenly think the orioles have left during the summer, but in fact, the birds are concentrating on finding insects to feed their young.

male

female

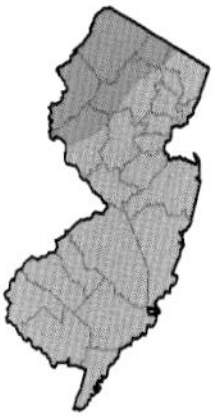

MIGRATION
WINTER

EVENING GROSBEAK
Coccothraustes vespertinus

Size: 8" (20 cm)

Male: A striking bird with a stocky body, large ivory-to-greenish bill, bright yellow eyebrows, a dirty yellow head, black-and-white wings and tail, and yellow rump and belly.

Female: similar to male, with softer colors, and gray head and throat

Juvenile: same as female, brown bill

Nest: cup; female builds; 1 brood per year

Eggs: 3-4; blue with brown markings

Incubation: 12-14 days; female incubates

Fledging: 13-14 days; female and male feed young

Migration: irruptive, seasonal movement brings birds to New Jersey during winter

Food: seeds, insects, fruit, comes to seed feeders

Compare: Larger than its close relative, the American Goldfinch (pg. 283). Look for the dark head with bright yellow eyebrow and extra large bill of the Evening Grosbeak.

Stan's Notes: One of the largest finches. Has characteristic undulating finch-like flight. Has unusually large bill for cracking seeds, its main source of food. Often seen on gravel roads eating gravel, from which it gets minerals, salts and grit to grind up seeds it eats. Moves in large flocks in winter. Sheds outer layer of its bill in spring, exposing blue green bill. More numerous in some years than others.

Eastern Meadowlark
Sturnella magna

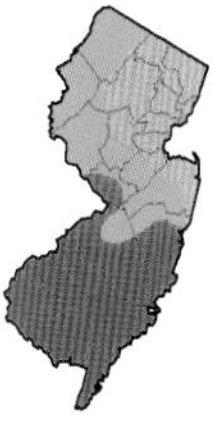

YEAR-ROUND
MIGRATION
SUMMER

Size: 9" (22.5 cm)

Male: A robin-shaped bird with brown back, lemon yellow chest and prominent black V-shaped necklace.White outer tail feathers.

Female: same as male

Juvenile: same as adult

Nest: cup, on the ground in dense cover; female builds; 2 broods per year

Eggs: 3-5; white with brown markings

Incubation: 13-15 days; female incubates

Fledging: 11-12 days; female and male feed young

Migration: complete, to Central America

Food: insects, seeds

Compare: The only large yellow bird with a black V mark on chest.

Stan's Notes: A bird of open grassy country. Best known for its wonderful song. Often seen perched on a fence post, it will quickly dive into tall grass when approached. Has conspicuous white markings on each side of its tail, most often seen when flying away. Nest is sometimes domed with dried grass. Called Meadowlark because it's a bird of meadows and sings like the larks of Europe. Eastern Meadowlark's song is a flute-like, clear whistle. Not a member of the lark family, it actually belongs to the blackbird family. Related to blackbirds, grackles and orioles.

HELPFUL RESOURCES:

Birder's Bug Book, The. Waldbauer, Gilbert. Cambridge: Harvard University Pres 1998.

Birder's Dictionary. Cox, Randall T. Helena, MT: Falcon Press Publishing, 199(

Birder's Handbook, The. Ehrlich, Paul, David S. Dobkin and Darryl Wheye. Ne York: Simon and Schuster, 1988.

Birds Do It, Too: The Amazing Sex Life of Birds. Harrison, George and Kit Harriso Minocqua, WI: Willow Creek Press, 1997.

Birds of Forest, Yard, and Thicket. Eastman, John. Mechanicsburg, PA: Stackpo Books, 1997.

Birds of New Jersey. Walsh, Joan, Vince Elia, Rich Kane and Thomas Halliwe Bernardsville: New Jersey Audubon Society, 1999.

Birds of North American Birds. Kaufman, Kenn. New York: Houghton Miffli 2000.

Blackbirds of the Americas. Orians, Gordon. Seattle: University of Washingtc Press, 1985.

Cardinal, The. Osborne, June. Austin: University of Texas Press, 1995.

Dictionary of American Bird Names, The. Choate, Ernest A. Boston: Harva Common Press, 1985.

Everything You Never Learned About Birds. Rupp, Rebecca. Pownal, VT: Stor Publishing, 1997.

Field Guide to the Birds, A: A Completely New Guide to All the Birds of Eastern an Central North America, Peterson, Roger Tory, and Virginia Marie Peterson. Boston: Houghton Mifflin Co., 1998.

Field Guide to the Birds of North America, Third Edition. Washington, DC: National Geographic Society, 1999.

Field Guide to Warblers of North America, A. Dunn, Jon and Kimball Garret Boston: Houghton Mifflin, 1997.

Folklore of Birds. Martin, Laura C. Old Saybrook, CT: Globe Pequot Press, 199

Guide to Bird Behavior, A: Vol I, II, III. Stokes, Donald and Lillian Stokes. Bosto Little, Brown and Company, 1989.

How Birds Migrate. Kerlinger, Paul. Mechanicsburg, PA: Stackpole Books, 1995

Lives of Birds, The: Birds of the World and Their Behavior. Short, Lester L. Colling dale, PA: DIANE Publishing, 2000.

Living on the Wind. Weidensaul, Scott. New York: North Point Press, 2000.

National Audubon Society, North American Birdfeeder Handbook. Burton, Rober New York: Dorling Kindersley Publishing, 1995.

Photographic Guide to North American Raptors, A. Wheeler, Brian K. and William S. Clark. New York: Academic Press, 1999.

Secret Lives of Birds, The. Gingras, Pierre. Toronto: Key Porter Books, 1997.

Secrets of the Nest. Dunning, Joan. Boston: Houghton Mifflin, 1994.

Stokes Bluebird Book: The Complete Guide to Attracting Bluebirds. Stokes, Donald and Lillian Stokes. Boston: Little Brown Co., 1991.

Stokes Field Guide to Birds: Eastern Region. Stokes, Donald and Lillian Stokes. Boston: Little, Brown and Company, 1996.

Stokes Purple Martin Book. Stokes, Donald and Lillian Stokes. Boston: Little, Brown and Company, 1997.

Sparrows and Buntings. Byers, Clive, Jon Curson and Urban Olsson. New York: Houghton Mifflin, 1995.

Swallows and Status and Distribution of New Jersey's Birds, The. Leck, Charles F. New Brunswick: Rutgers University Press, 1984.

New Jersey Birding Hotlines. To hear a recording of where birds have been seen, call these prerecorded hotlines:

Cape May 609-861-0466
Statewide 908-766-2661

Web Pages:

The Internet has become a valuable place to learn about birds. The following are a few web sites that will assist you in your pursuit of birds. You might find birding on the net a fun way to learn more about birds or to spend a long winter night.

SITE	ADDRESS
National Audubon Society of New Jersey	www.audubon.org/chapter/nj
American Birding Association	www.americanbirding.org
Cornell Lab of Ornithology	www.birds.cornell.edu
Author Stan Tekiela's home page	www.naturesmart.com

About the Author:

Stan Tekiela is a naturalist, author and wildlife photographer with a Bachelor of Science degree in Natural History from the University of Minnesota. He has been a professional naturalist for over 20 years and is a member of the Minnesota Naturalist Association, the Outdoor Writers Association of America and Canon Professional Services. Stan actively studies and photographs birds throughout the U.S. He received an Excellence in Interpretation award from the National Association for Interpretation, and a regional award for Commitment to Outdoor Education. A columnist and radio personality, his syndicated column appears in more than 20 cities and he can be heard on a number of radio stations. Stan resides in Victoria, Minnesota, with wife Katherine and daughter Abigail. He can be contacted via his web page at www.naturesmart.com.

Stan authors several field guides for other states including guides for birds, birds of prey, wildflowers and trees.